Teaching Fairly
in an
Unfair World

Kathleen Gould Lundy

Pembroke Publishers Limited

For My Mother

© 2008 Pembroke Publishers
538 Hood Road
Markham, Ontario, Canada L3R 3K9
www.pembrokepublishers.com

Distributed in the U.S. by Stenhouse Publishers
480 Congress Street
Portland, ME 04101
www.stenhouse.com

We acknowledge the financial support of the Government of Canada through the Book Publishing Industry Development Program (BPIDP) for our publishing activities.

We acknowledge the assistance of the Government of Ontario through the Ontario Media Development Corporation's Ontario Book Initiative.

Library and Archives Canada Cataloguing in Publication

Lundy, Kathleen Gould
   Teaching fairly in an unfair world / Kathleen Gould Lundy.

Includes index.
ISBN 978-1-55138-231-9

   1. Mixed ability grouping in education. 2. Inclusive education. 3. Active learning. 4. Multicultural education. I. Title.

LC1200.L86 2008   71.2'52   C2008-903755-3

Editor: Jane McNulty
Cover Design: John Zehethofer
Typesetting: Jay Tee Graphics Ltd.

Printed and bound in Canada
9 8 7 6 5 4 3 2

ANCIENT FOREST™ FRIENDLY

39 trees were saved for our forests

Preserving our environment
Pembroke Publishers chose to print the pages of this book on recycled paper and saved these resources¹:

energy	water	greenhouse gases	solid waste
12 million BTUs	67,286 L	1,674 kg	490 kg

Printed by **Webcom Inc.** on Legacy Hi-Bulk White 100% post-consumer waste.

FSC
Mixed Sources
Product group from well-managed forests, controlled sources and recycled wood or fiber
Cert no. SW-COC-002358
www.fsc.org
© 1996 Forest Stewardship Council

¹Estimates were made using the Environmental Defense Paper Calculator.

Contents

Preface   5

1. Classrooms as Places of Possibility   8

Being Mindful of Our Power   9
Rethinking What and How We Teach   9
What Do Teachers Who Teach Fairly Do?   10
Recognizing and Meeting the Needs of All Students   11
Unlocking the Future for Our Students   11
Distinguishing Fairness from Unfairness for Ourselves and for Others   12
Teachers Make a Difference   14
Imagine a School…   15
A Teacher's Sense of Students and Students' Sense of Themselves   21

2. What Do We Mean by an Inclusive Curriculum?   23

An Inclusive and Equitable School Environment   25
The Importance of Courageous Leadership   27
Collegiality, Collaboration, and Mentorship   27
Imagining Yourself Forward   29

3. Building Community   32

Creating Community: Moving Beyond Estrangement and Alienation   33
New Beginnings: I See…, I Wonder…, I Hope…   33
The Six Es of Effective Teaching   35
Keep Expectations High   36
Establish an Inclusive, Respectful Environment for Learning   36
"Protecting Our Students Into Understanding"   51

4. Critical Thinking and Emotional Literacy (Elementary)   52

Drama, Empathy, and Point of View   53
Exploring Silent Voices Through Drama   54
Drama and Equity Education   56
The Woman Who Outshone the Sun   58
Architecture of the Imagination   60
The Arrival   64
In a Class of Her Own   70
The Giver   75
Nobody Rides the Unicorn   79
Encounter   82

5. Interpreting Text Through Active Engagement (Secondary)   89

Residential Schools: The Stolen Years   90
The Island   92

Angelica-Leslie   *96*
"The Man Who Finds That His Son Has Become a Thief"   *102*
"Letter"   *106*
The Elephant Man   *110*
 "Wedding Album"   *114*
The Diary of Anne Frank   *121*

6. Remaining Hopeful   *126*

Deciding What to Hope For   *127*
Professional Learning Communities   *128*
Shining Threads of Hope   *128*
The Context in Which We Live and Teach   *129*
Collaboration Versus Competition   *130*
Collegiality   *130*
What *Can* I Control?   *131*
Constructing Together   *131*

50 Teaching Strategies to Use in an Inclusive Classroom   *134*

Blackline Masters   *146*

Bibliography   *151*

Index   *155*

Acknowledgements   *159*

Preface

The real voyage of discovery consists not in seeking new landscapes but in having new eyes. — Marcel Proust

June was suddenly upon us. I was wrapping up a drama project with a Grade 8 class in an inner city school in Toronto. I had begun the project in March and had spent a fair amount of time with this class, made up of thirty-six students from seventeen different countries around the world. I thought that I knew most of the students well. The teacher and I shared our delight in the accomplishments of the students as they worked through various drama techniques that helped them grow into articulate, passionate actors who had important stories to tell about bullying and what to do about it.

We had persevered in tackling some common issues and problems that young adolescents confront in school. There had been misunderstandings and difficult negotiations, but we had done some good work together. Although pressed for time, we had squeezed a number of workshops into a very busy curriculum and now we were on our last lap together. Everyone was excited about the performance that was going to take place that afternoon in front of the rest of the middle school students in the school cafeteria.

I arrived at the school just before the bell rang. There was the usual commotion that signals the beginning of a school day during the hot days of June. Lots of laughter and physical energy filled the hallways. I saw the homeroom teacher standing outside her classroom talking to Michael, a student who was popular with everyone in the class. A boy named Fahim approached Michael just as the teacher was interrupted by a colleague.

Fahim and Michael were good friends and spent most of their time together.

The teacher had turned away momentarily and before Fahim could speak, Michael commented on Fahim's new haircut. He said, "Look at you, man. You look like a terrorist." Fahim appeared confused. Michael continued, "You look like a terrorist; your haircut—it makes you look like a terrorist…." Fahim looked devastated, said nothing, and quickly disappeared into the classroom. The teacher finished speaking to her colleague and turned back to Michael. She had not observed what had just taken place between the two boys.

I entered the classroom. Time was tight—we only had a few hours before the final performance. As the students started to rearrange the desks to make room for the work we were about to do, I spoke to the teacher about the interaction between the two boys in the hallway. I could see Fahim out of the corner of my eye. He was standing by himself, not participating in any way. Usually, he was engaged and helpful in class. I wondered aloud whether we should resolve the issue between Fahim and Michael privately because I felt that we could not continue until Michael's comment had been dealt with. The teacher regarded me with a certain degree of impatience. She had had the students released from their morning classes and we had so little time to get things ready. Couldn't this wait?

I could see her point. Wasn't this just a minor incident? Why take time out of a very busy morning to wrestle with it? Couldn't we let it go—just this once?

I relented. After all, I was a guest in the school and I, too, was feeling the pressure of the impending performance. So we began to rehearse, but Fahim—who played a key role in the collective drama—participated listlessly. I could tell that he was suffering. He had been enormously hurt by his friend and he was at a loss as to how to handle it.

After the rehearsal, the teacher—who had recognized as soon as the rehearsal began that the tension between Michael and Fahim had to be diffused—suggested that we meet with both boys. We bought lunch for the two students in the cafeteria and then met in a room near the school office. We were about to present a play about bullying and its impact on victims and onlookers. The irony of that fact was not lost on any of us. The teacher, who had worked in the school for a long time, patiently asked the boys to explain to her what had transpired between them.

It became clear that Michael had no idea how hurtful his comment had been. He began by insisting that the haircut *did* make Fahim look like the headshots of terrorists that he had seen on TV. He did not know what the "big deal" was.

In response, Fahim, who is of Pakistani heritage, told us about how his father was regularly called "Osama bin there done that" at work and about how his sister had had her headscarf pulled off her head while attending high school right after 9/11. He said that more and more people were making unacceptable connections between his Islamic heritage and global terrorism and that he and his family were sick of being victimized. He was completely mortified that Michael, whom he considered one of his best friends, could hurt his feelings in such a way.

Clearly, Michael had not realized how devastated Fahim was and how insulting his words had been to his friend. We spent some time talking about preconceptions that had been planted in Michael's mind due to media influences. He was unaware of how he had been swayed by certain biased images on television. Now, however, he was willing to challenge some myths promoted by the media. The teacher reminded Michael of all the work that he and his classmates had done together in Media Literacy to deconstruct images of racism. She and Michael shared the same Jamaican-Canadian heritage. Michael was fully aware of how hurtful racism is. In fact, he told some of his own stories about his brother being discriminated against at work.

For my part, I, a white woman, was fully aware that I was bearing witness to something that people of color deal with in a white-dominated society all the time. There were a lot of tears and a quiet sadness enveloped us. We were four people struggling to come to terms with how difficult it is to live in the world.

I can't remember all the things that we talked about in that hour as the teacher generously shared her apple and cookies and provided lots of tissues, while being strong and direct and fair. But I do remember this. At the end of the conversation, Michael looked at all of us and said: "In order to stop hurting people, you need to know SO much about SO many things. It's kind of overwhelming...." The teacher and I looked into the eyes of the two boys and thought about all the hard work and exploration of issues that we had done together as a class through drama. Even though we were scheduled to perform as a team that afternoon, there was still so much more we needed to know about one another and the world in which we live if we were going to get things right.

This is one of the stories about my experiences working in schools that made me want to write this book. I agree with Michael. This kind of work *is* overwhelming and it will never be "done." There is so much to learn about so many things. There are no easy solutions and, sometimes, no clear answers at all to some of the questions that we grapple with when teaching about fairness. I have struggled to write about ways to teach about fairness and ways to teach fairly, but I realize that I myself still have so much to learn and can only keep trying to do things in the best way possible.

More and more of us work in culturally, racially, and linguistically diverse classrooms. Some of us teach in economically disadvantaged school settings. No matter where we teach, we know how important it is to build relationships with our students and to gain their respect. But we have to do more than what we have been doing. We need to make the time in a crowded curriculum to talk with our students about who they are, where they are from, what they want to accomplish, and how they want to live in the world. We need to have the courage to set up inclusive classrooms in which students feel safe to talk about controversial issues and to explore what Deborah Britzman and Alice Pitt, two of my colleagues at York University's Faculty of Education, call "difficult knowledge."

We need to engage in our own personal, critical reflections upon our life stories so that we recognize certain things about ourselves: our fears, our privilege, and our assumptions. We need to remember how important it is to help our students construct knowledge about the world together as they participate in challenging, open-ended, imaginative, intellectual, and artistic pursuits from various perspectives. Furthermore, in a global economy in which so much pressure is placed on the individual—through tests and other competitive factors—we need to help our students learn to become critically aware of what is fair not only for themselves but for others. Most important of all, we need to summon the courage to cancel the dress rehearsals when real life takes over and when hurtful encounters disrupt the community that we call the classroom. I want us to give ourselves permission and time to mend broken hearts through thoughtful, empathetic discussion so that important teaching and learning can proceed.

1

Classrooms as Places of Possibilities

> No one has realized the wealth of sympathy, the kindness and generosity hidden in the soul of a child. The effort of every true education should be to unlock that treasure. — Emma Goldman

This book is for teachers with adventurous spirits: those who are willing to make connections with their students to nurture relationships based on mutual respect; those who are confident enough to rely on their intuition as well as what they know about teaching and learning and who deftly make program changes when they need to; and those who know that the rhythm of teaching is dependent on active, careful listening to student voices—not only voices that are heard but also those that have been silent for too long.

This is a book about teaching fairly as well as a book that provides ways of teaching about fairness. Teachers will learn how to think in new ways about inclusive curriculum, create respectful environments in their classrooms, and reach out to the communities that surround the school. They will be encouraged to help their students recognize unfairness, question their assumptions, adopt multiple perspectives, and challenge themselves to think critically about social justice and injustice. They will learn how to encourage students to routinely question what they think of as normal and to ask difficult questions that sometimes have multiple answers. Teachers will also learn how to help students find their voices to tell important stories that need to be shared.

The teacher's job in public education has always been about fairness. As we teach, we are intent on eliminating bias, preventing discrimination, and maintaining high expectations of excellence for every student who walks through the doors of our classrooms. Why do we strive so hard to make sure that teaching works and that learning matters? Because we want our students to get caught up in the full current of life—both in school and beyond—and to make good choices for the future. We want them to lead lives that are privately happy and publicly useful. We want them to grasp onto hope as they grow and learn despite the difficulties that lie in their paths. In order for them to pursue a life worth living, they need to be resilient and positive.

Teachers make an enormous difference in the lives of students simply on the basis of how and what they teach. We need to be aware of what many equity educators term the "location" of our students in terms of their identities and to work with curriculum that is responsive to their needs and interests. We must also strive to know and understand the communities in which our students live and to recognize how gender, race, ethnicity, immigrant status, social class, urban/rural context, national origin, sexual orientation, and linguistic backgrounds shape interactions in the classroom. Finally, it is crucial for teachers to unpack their own stories of identity and to be aware of how their privilege and power influence the classroom dynamic.

Being Mindful of Our Power

We teachers have enormous power to influence the future of the students in our care. We need to be mindful of that power and remain consistently conscious of what it means to teach fairly in an unfair world. Gaining students' trust and enlisting their cooperation are essential if we are going to succeed in the kind of critical work around social issues that is necessary in today's world.

We have to continually "check ourselves" by self-monitoring what we are saying, thinking, feeling, and doing in the classrooms and hallways of our schools. We need to be cognizant of our students' reactions and realities and know when to change direction if necessary, while approaching tasks with sensitivity and discretion. For example, during the month-long Muslim religious observance of Ramadan, non-Muslims in the school might consult with Muslim colleagues and students to learn more about this important aspect of Muslim life. Since many Muslim colleagues and students fast during Ramadan, teachers must take into account how this might influence everyday practice in their classrooms.

In a course on Urban Diversity taught in the Faculty of Education at York University in Toronto, Carl James encourages his teacher candidates to recognize that the racism that is inherent in educational structures must be labeled and addressed directly: "Critical educators make explicit the contradictions and paradoxes that are inherent in institutions, such as schools, which promise equality and inclusivity while producing and reproducing inequalities based on race, class, gender and other factors." (James, 2004) James is intent on inviting marginalized students into a learning process in which their "difference" does not act as a barrier to active engagement in their own learning.

Rethinking What and How We Teach

Teachers begin with a set of core beliefs about teaching and learning in the democratic classroom and then modify these beliefs as they encounter their students and learn from them. In my classes at the Faculty of Education at York University, I encourage my student teachers to examine critically the activities they are constructing for and with their students, and to stay open to rethinking what they ask of their students as well as what teaching strategies and interventions they select. I also ask them to be mindful of who they are in terms of their own identities and privilege.

Most of my student teachers were successful in school. Sometimes this makes it difficult for them to empathize with those who find learning challenging. For the most part, my student teachers grew up in middle class circumstances or, if they did not, their profession will allow them to attain a certain privileged status in society. I tell them that it is vital, therefore, that they develop awareness of realities other than their own. For instance, it might be difficult for some students to stay after school for extra help if they have to babysit younger siblings; five dollars for admission to a play is a lot of money for some students; a donation to a food bank might be impossible for certain students. Demanding that homework be done on a computer can also cause problems, as can asking students to hold hands, look us in the eye, dress in a certain way, or keep a second pair of shoes in their lockers so that the classroom floor stays clean. These are examples of the many things that might cause some students to feel uncomfortable for various cultural or socio-economic reasons.

What Do Teachers Who Teach Fairly Do?

What are the characteristics and behaviors of a teacher who teaches fairly? Teachers who value and nurture a respectful classroom environment based on principles of fairness interact with their students in the following ways:

- They communicate ideas and instructions clearly.
- They guide and limit behavior to keep students safe.
- They expect all of their students to be successful.
- They encourage their students to be the best they can be on that particular day.
- They mentor their students in order to show them how to live in the world.
- They help students to question the construction and understanding of difference.
- They are open to new ideas and ways of approaching teaching and learning.
- They validate the experiences of all their students, by finding source material in the curriculum that acts as a mirror for the students' own identities.
- They engage students in critical thinking by means of which they come to question and understand their relationships to their community, their society, and the world.
- They ensure that their student' needs, interests, and aspirations are met not only through curriculum, resources, pedagogy, and educational programs, but also through time spent together in the classroom.
- They help students examine their lives to understand their own personal histories.
- They listen and watch for those students who remain silent.
- They celebrate their students' successes.
- They know that learning takes time, so they rehearse and practice new skills.
- They "protect their students into understanding." (For more about this approach, see Chapter 3.)
- They wear their profession in public.
- They view learning about teaching as never-ending.
- They value where their students are from, both in terms of their communities and the broader social context and they remain mindful of that context so that teaching works and learning matters.

Recognizing and Meeting the Needs of All Students

A Life Worth Living

Time Somebody told Me
How they loved and needed me
How my smile is filled with hope
   and my spirit sets them free
How my eyes shine, full of light
How good they feel when
they hug me tight
Time Somebody told Me
So, I had a talk with myself
Just me, nobody else
'Cause it was time
Somebody told Me

Quantedius Hall
12 years old

"Think about a time when you were completely safe and happy—when everything in your life was fine…." So began a storytelling workshop that I was coordinating at a Dramatic Arts Festival for students from several high schools in Toronto. Approximately 25 secondary students were working with a professional storyteller in one of many workshops and this was how the storyteller began her session. The workshop space was a room in the basement of a downtown church. I had popped in to make sure that things were running smoothly. The students hailed from schools all across the city and they had just met each other. They were quiet and thoughtful about the task at hand and they had obediently closed their eyes. The storyteller then asked the students to open their eyes, get into groups of three, introduce themselves to each other, and tell their stories to one another. A tall, redheaded student approached the storyteller and me as the groups were assembling. "The problem is," he admitted, "I can't remember a time when I ever felt this way…."

I have never forgotten that moment in my teaching career. I remember the pain in that young boy's eyes and I was struck by the confusion and shame he must have felt when he left his group and approached us. In that moment, I realized that preparing lessons and workshops out of context could be a dangerous act. One cannot plan a lesson adequately without first knowing what kinds of experiences our students are bringing to the learning encounter. We need to recognize who our students are and where they are from before we plan what it is they need to know and how they are going to learn it. Carl James has since taught me that teachers "need to think critically of the contexts in which we teach, the subjectivities that we bring to our work and the assumptions that we have of our students." (James, 2004). Only when we honor this principle can we move forward.

We have a huge responsibility to establish classrooms as places of possibility where students feel safe, honored, excited, challenged, and hopeful about the work that lies before them. We need to affirm the life experiences of the students whom we meet in our classrooms and in the hallways of our schools and to acknowledge that schools are more than just places where teachers teach and students learn. We need to maintain the core belief that schools are places where intellects expand, where social/emotional learning takes place, where attitudes about living in the world are challenged and transformed, and where hopeful dreams are born and thrive.

Unlocking the Future for Our Students

The Toronto District School Board's Equity Foundation Statement claims that the board is "committed to ensuring that fairness, equity, and inclusion are essential principles of our school system and are integrated into all our policies, programs, operations and practices." This board's teachers are encouraged to acquire an understanding of the issues that are embedded in the social and cultural contexts in which their schools function. Board policies underscore our need to understand what our students are up against and to work towards unlocking the future for them.

As in many jurisdictions, Toronto schools are held accountable for ensuring students' success on tests at the Grades 3, 6, and 9 levels. Yet many schools, not only in Toronto but also across Canada, face numerous challenges in providing a quality education for all students. One such challenge arises from children living in homes in which both parents work several jobs to provide food and shelter for their families and in which children are not given appropriate supervision after school. Some schools have families who live in cars or motels. Many parents struggle to pay bills because of the meagre wages they receive from low-paying jobs. All of these social, physical, and emotional circumstances greatly impact student learning.

Despite the best of intentions, some schools contribute to systemic biases in terms of class and race. I have observed this bias firsthand. I remember sitting in an office in a school waiting for a team of artists to arrive so that I could work with them in a classroom. We had been guest participants for a number of weeks in an interdisciplinary arts project. I watched from my chair in the office as a number of Grade 8 boys whom I had taught came into the office, half-carrying a friend who had fallen and hurt himself in the playground. I watched the boys as they sought the help of the school secretary. They stood around their friend, joking and encouraging him as the secretary cleaned the blood from the wound and applied a cold compress. Later, I told one of the teachers in the school how impressed I had been by how the students took care of their injured friend. I think I said something about how I saw these students as real leaders in the future—prime ministers, business leaders, doctors, social workers. My colleague looked at me disparagingly and replied, "Forget it. These students don't stand a chance given where they live and what they come from."

We cannot teach unless we believe that our work will make a difference in the lives of our students. Wangari Maathi, the Nobel Peace Prize winner who, against all odds, established the Green Belt movement in Kenya, has helped me understand that there are three ways in which we can view our current reality. We can possess what she calls "poverty thinking" that allows us to fall into an inevitable future. Second, we can hang on to what she terms "probability thinking" and foresee only our predictable future. In other words, we adopt the belief that we can do nothing to change how things are in the world. Maathi encourages us to move beyond these restricting mindsets into a third realm: "possibility thinking." In this mode of thinking, we become enamored of and attached to our preferred future. Teachers committed to unlocking the future for their students make a habit of modeling "possibility thinking."

We can work together for a better world with men and women of goodwill, those who radiate the intrinsic goodness of humankind. To do so effectively, the world needs a global ethic with values which give meaning to life experiences and, more than religious institutions and dogmas, sustain the non-material dimension of humanity. Mankind's universal values of love, compassion, solidarity, caring and tolerance should form the basis for this global ethic which should permeate culture, politics, trade, religion and philosophy. It should also permeate the extended family of the United Nations.

Wangari Maathi

Distinguishing Fairness from Unfairness for Ourselves and for Others

We need to teach our students well—to provide them with the thinking tools they need to wrestle with facts and figures so they can become critically aware of how the world works on many levels. But we also need to teach them how to live in the world as ethical citizens. We need to help our students learn to discern what is fair not just for themselves but also for others, and to develop self-awareness of how their actions can either benefit or damage themselves or others. This mental stance requires them to distinguish what is fair from what is unfair, to be able to hold many different ideas in their heads at once, and to make choices that benefit others as well as themselves.

Educating Students to Be Good Citizens

The work that I do with students in the classroom allows them to become actively engaged with ideas, themes, relationships, characters, historical and contemporary incidents, images, and texts from the inside out. Through drama and other kinds of interactive activities, I encourage students to cooperate with one another, express their emotions, seek alternative solutions to problems, engage in conflict resolution, and participate fully in the making of individual and collective meaning. By means of these activities, I hope that students will develop respect for themselves and for others as they experience firsthand what life must be like for people who are different from themselves. As I teach material that requires students to collaborate with each other, I monitor the ways in which students develop a more positive self-image. As the material we are exploring introduces new perspectives, I watch to see if my students are becoming more comfortable in acknowledging, accepting, understanding, and celebrating human differences. In the end, I hope that they will acquire a sense of social responsibility as well as a sense of justice for themselves as well as for others.

Goethe tells us that "character develops in quiet places." To develop one's character, one requires, among other things, time to experiment with new ideas and experience life in many different ways; to participate in thoughtful dialogue with an empathetic mentor who does not judge but guides and asks significant questions; to interact with others who don't necessarily hold the same view of the world; and to encounter literature, art, ideas, facts, and opinions that trigger new understandings. The classroom is a central place where students develop and grow as human beings. Their character is shaped by what happens both at home, in the community, and at school. Teachers exert an enormous influence on their students' character development by how and what they teach.

Elliot Eisner, Professor Emeritus of Art and Education at Stanford University, tells us that children are born with brains and it is up to us as teachers to shape their brains into minds. We want our students to be mindful of others' opinions and feelings. As they interact with one another and discuss difficult concepts, we need to help them learn to hold many different thoughts in their minds—to live with ambiguity and not be afraid of it—until they reach a decision, solve a problem, or learn to live with the many facets of a difficult issue.

"Character" is a word that is charged with many meanings in educational circles. Many school districts are attempting to implement a curriculum that teaches students about values such as Respect, Responsibility, Honesty, Integrity, Empathy, Fairness, Initiative, Perseverance, Courage, and Optimism. I know from years of teaching experience how difficult it is for some students to remain optimistic when things are falling apart at home; how hard it is for them to be empathetic towards others when they do not feel good about themselves; and how challenging it is to be responsible and caring when developmentally they are still very immature. I am interested in educating students to be good people—good to others and good to themselves. I am aware of the challenges that exist in every classroom, but I believe that there are many ways to accomplish this goal:

1. We need to create a school culture in which all people—teachers, parents, students, and others—model the qualities of respect, responsibility, and caring.

It is the mark of an educated mind to be able to entertain a thought without accepting it.

Aristotle

If there is light in the soul, there
will be beauty in the person.
If there is beauty in the person,
there will be harmony in the
house.
If there is harmony in the house,
there will be order in the nation.
If there is order in the nation,
there will be peace in the world.

Chinese proverb

2. As teachers, we need to be aware of our own privilege and power, really listen to what our students are telling us about who they are and how they learn best, and use appropriate teaching techniques.
3. The work that we do with students has to matter. Pedagogical content has to be relevant to our students' lives and they have to care about learning this content.
4. The way in which we teach should be imaginative and open-ended. It should allow the students to go "inside the experience" so that they have the opportunity to unpack the material in critical, respectful, and imaginative ways. As teachers, we need to find ways to engage our students actively with difficult and layered material, and teach them imaginative and artful ways to represent their new understandings.
5. We must help students become resilient and confident so that they can be successful. I have never thought of school as a place to get students ready for life ahead. School *is* life. School is not a rehearsal and students need to be nurtured and cared for and challenged and taught in order to prepare them for the lives they are living in the *present*.

Teachers Make a Difference

Many years ago I had the opportunity of working with a Grade 6 class at Hughes Public School in downtown Toronto. The school is now closed, but I remember the beautiful, wide, polished hardwood floors on the third floor of the building, the eager students who were mostly from immigrant backgrounds, and the dedicated staff and principal who collaborated so well with each other. The school was experiencing declining enrollment—which is why it was eventually closed —but the small size of the student body allowed the teachers to get to know every student and to work together on projects that were very exciting. The principal delighted in the strength and expertise of her staff and supported them in all their endeavors.

I remember working in the library with the Grade 6 students on a drama based on a storybook called *The Sea People* (now out of print). The work that the students had done in interpreting the story through drama and movement was exceptional. Even more thrilling were the follow-up discussions about the unjust king and the effect that his rulings had on the people of the Small Island. I remember stopping at one point in the discussion and asking the students if this kind of creative work and deep reflection was typical of the kinds of interactions that happened in their classroom on a daily basis. The students replied that it was. I then asked them, "Why do you conduct yourselves with such decorum and sensitivity?" All the students turned around and pointed at their teacher. "He demands this of us," declared one girl. Other students explained that the teacher expected boys and girls to work together, to resolve conflicts with his help, and to take responsibility for establishing a classroom atmosphere that was free from strife.

Research tells us that the disposition of the teacher is of paramount importance in promoting learning. Successful teachers demonstrate a positive attitude but they are not Pollyannas; they set high expectations for all of their students but they take underlying problems into account and are empathetic to students' varying needs and circumstances. Good teachers develop the confidence to seek out support, advice, and guidance from colleagues and mentors in order to deal with difficult situations. They are willing to work with others to assess their programs on a regular basis and they strive energetically to find answers to complex problems. No matter what obstacles they face, they continue to teach with skill and with grace.

Imagine a School...

I will describe an experience that has profoundly influenced the way in which I think about education, about the dynamics of teaching and learning, and about teacher-student relationships. This experience helped to cement my understanding of classrooms (both literal and metaphorical) as places of possibility.

In May 2006, the Canadian Education Association organized a symposium for educational leaders in Vancouver based on the theme "Getting it Right for Adolescent Learners." The CEA wanted to investigate schooling from the perspective of learning and the association therefore invited high school students from three Canadian cities (Halifax, Toronto, and Vancouver) to the symposium. Students from these schools were asked to create and present a dramatic anthology based on their personal stories of school experiences. To be staged on the first night of the symposium, the presentation would serve to spark constructive conversations about the purpose and format of schooling for adolescent learners.

I was invited to be the project's artistic director. The process of building the play was one of the most exciting challenges of my teaching career. At the time, I was in the midst of setting up a program at York University called "Destination Arts," a joint venture of the Faculties of Education and Fine Arts that was intended to foster partnerships among artists, arts organizations, faculty, teacher candidates, graduate students, teachers, school administrators, and community members. I saw the CEA's venture as a perfect complement to the Destination Arts program. Thus, York University partnered with the CEA and the three Canadian school boards. We enlisted the aid of my husband, Chuck Lundy, an award-winning educational film director, to create two DVDs, one depicting the process and one depicting the performance itself, based on videotapes produced by the student participants.

The directors and superintendents of education in the three boards chose the participating schools: Templeton High School in Vancouver, Bloor Collegiate Institute in Toronto, and Prince Andrew High School in Halifax. All the students—nine from each school (eight actors and one videographer)—were enrolled in drama classes and most were in Grade 12. I had specifically asked that the students selected represent the various populations of the three cities, and therefore the group was racially, ethnically, economically, and academically diverse. Because I was interested in hearing voices that are often unheard, I did not want only those students who were performing well academically to participate in the project. For that reason, many of the participants were students who struggled in school for various reasons.

Launching the Project

The first meeting with the teachers from the three cities, which took place at the Faculty of Destination Arts at York University, was key to establishing a cooperative working relationship. We spent one full day sharing information about the students and planning the project along with representatives from the CEA and York University and our video director. We wanted students to imagine new realities and to answer a key question: "What could high schools look like if we got it right?" To help them formulate an answer, I proposed that we situate the drama work around the theme "articulation of voice."

Initial Explorations and Rehearsals

In March we began working with the students. Because we did not have much time, I knew I had to find effective ways to gain insight into the details of their lives in secondary schools and to probe deeply enough inside that human experience to find the voices we needed to hear.

The first, most important job when the group met was to establish trust, collaboration, and respect. I divided students from the three schools into small groups. I wanted first of all to discover how the students defined their identities in relationship to their school environments and to their neighborhoods. In an exercise called "I am From…/We are From…" (see page 44), students wrote personal stories describing their identities, family background, academic challenges, and so on. Using various drama exercises, the three groups began to form a community of learners, all willing to engage in the difficult work of revealing their true feelings about what was happening in their schools.

Next, students were asked to tell a story about a critical moment in their school experience—perhaps one related to a time when they had made a mistake and thought differently about themselves afterwards, or one related to a relationship that had gone awry. They told these stories in small groups and then began to elaborate on them through improvisation. They explored ways to "get these stories up on their feet" in order to share them with the larger group. Because they employed the common language of drama, they worked well together. Some of their stories were heartbreaking; others were inspirational; all showed courage.

I had invited my fourth-year theatre and pre-service education students to participate in this exercise so that they could witness the teaching and learning that can occur through drama. The pre-service students were amazed by the enthusiasm and creativity of the high school students and delighted to witness the activities presented in their university courses come to life through the improvisations of the high school learners. Any doubts that they might have had about creative drama teaching immediately flew out the window as they observed its impact on the younger students.

As we worked together in this university setting—listening to the voices of academics, engaging in conversations with representatives from the CEA, receiving support from student teachers and theatre students—the high school students became intrigued by the possibility that the re-enactment of their stories might trigger a large enough response with a national audience to make changes in their schools possible.

After the two-day rehearsals at York University, the students from Bloor Collegiate Institute confided to their drama teacher that they had never felt so empowered. Being treated like professionals—enjoying lunch and coffee breaks with teachers and receiving thanks for their work from adults who valued their contributions—affected them deeply and began to change the way they thought about themselves and their school. When the invitation to participate had first arrived from the CEA, the reaction from one of the Bloor students had been,

"Why would they choose a ghetto school like this one?" Later, however, as the project progressed, the school staff began to notice changes in the students' behavior. They were walking taller, showing more generosity toward others, smiling more, and showing more interest in schoolwork.

Developing the Play

Following the rehearsals, the drama teachers and the high school students returned home, where they continued to develop the play, using the personal stories they had generated as well as source material I had given them. When I visited the three schools in April, we continued to explore ways to provoke conversations and to represent material dramatically. We rehearsed Readers Theatre pieces, developed choreography, prepared improvisations, wrote two-voice poems, composed a rap, and created personal monologues. The students from Halifax co-composed a song with a professional songwriter. The students from Toronto wrote an "Imagine a School" poem, inspired by a Toronto student's keynote speech presented at a conference of educators. The Vancouver students wrote poetic monologues to tell individual stories of personal struggles in school. The drama teachers spent rehearsal time with the students both before and after my visits, and we stayed in regular contact with each other.

The work was difficult, but I never doubted that it would come together beautifully. The effort evolved a *karma* of its own—and people were generous in ways that surprised me. I was touched by the fact that in each of the cities, the directors, superintendents, and principals showed up not only to watch rehearsals, but also to meet and talk with the students, to listen to them, and to ask questions that validated the students' experiences. The students were thrilled that their work was given such attention. It was "pretty amazing," as one student put it, that not only the principal but also the board's director and superintendents dropped by to see the rehearsals.

Showtime!

Just two months after our first gathering, the company of actors and teachers reconvened in Vancouver on the Friday before the Monday evening performance. I was in the hotel lobby when the Toronto and Halifax students checked into the Delta Vancouver Suites. The reunion of the students from Toronto and Halifax was magical. After the hugs and the laughter, Leroy, a Toronto student, exclaimed, "Miss, that whole experience was beautiful—and I mean with two L's!" Many of these young people had never stayed in a hotel, and I was delighted by the welcome that the hotel staff extended to the students. Cookies and a respectful attitude were all part of the warm reception.

On Saturday, intensive rehearsals began. Jet lag had hit (the Vancouver students' grad dance had been the night before!) but everyone was "pumped." We knew our job was to encourage dialogue so that the Canadian school experience could be made better for adolescents. We knew that we had very little time to find an artistic way to weave together the various threads of conversations and storytelling developed thus far. We knew we wanted the audience to attend to the details—to listen to the stories and to be moved by them. We knew that we had to iron out how to say what we needed to say, not only provocatively but also respectfully. And, most of all, we knew we had to tell the truth.

From the beginning, the students were extremely focused. They took few breaks, but it didn't seem to matter. Their work ethic was remarkable.

After two and a half days in Vancouver, following long rehearsals that included finding transitions, ironing out sequencing, sharing new ideas, editing, and singing, the students were ready. That night, they opened the conference with their hour-long anthology. When it concluded, the audience stood, applauded, cheered, and wept.

What Did the Student Actors Tell Us?

What did the students who participated in the drama tell us ultimately? In some ways, you had to be there…. The medium really *was* the message. The students showed us how words and drama can send powerful signals to an audience:

1. **Good teachers make all the difference.** Students shared story after story of amazing teachers who went the extra mile, who believed in them and their potential, and who made positive futures possible. Because of their teachers' guidance and encouragement, students succeeded academically and socially.
2. **Allow us to make mistakes.** A school should be a place of experimentation, where mistakes are expected rather than penalized.
3. **Don't overwhelm us.** Students felt overwhelmed by the amount of work that was expected of them at one time and wished teachers would confer with their colleagues to balance the workload.
4. **Extra-curricular activities are important.** All the students agreed that extra-curricular activities are an essential part of the high school experience and wished that teachers would receive public recognition for the time and effort they devote to students outside the classroom.
5. **Respect us.** One student reminded us that teachers are not "nobles" and underlined the need for teachers to create a respectful classroom environment in which all voices are heard and in which power struggles are minimized. One student, who had attended six different high schools in three years, told us that only when the teachers and administrators saw beyond his reputation and gave him a chance did he begin to succeed.
6. **Teach us.** The cry for interesting, open-ended, relevant, and imaginative teaching was a key message. "The important thing about teachers is that they teach," commented Katie, one of the students in the production. From students in all three cities came stories of frustration about teachers who simply told students to open their textbooks and "do the work." There was frustration, too, that often the "good" teachers did all the "interesting stuff" with the smart kids, while giving the average students less stimulating, less exciting, and less dynamic curriculum to tackle.
7. **Don't make assumptions about us without getting to know us.** Immigrant students wanted their teachers to understand how difficult the transition from their countries of origin to Canada had been, and to acknowledge these trying experiences. In one scene, two students combined their voices in a poem to tell about the need to work hard to keep food on the table and a smile on the faces of their siblings. One student actor, who worked a regular shift cleaning banks from midnight until 8 a.m., was told constantly by teachers: "Come prepared [to class] or do not come at all." Another student had dreamt for years about the prom

dress that she would wear at her graduation. To save money for the dress, she had to work extra hours at a part-time job to make her dream come true. All of these obligations eat into school time, students explained, and teachers need to be sensitive to the realities of the lives of students outside of school.

8. **We are vulnerable.** Students told stories of pregnancy, thoughts of suicide, difficulty making friends, discouragement in the face of a tough curriculum, and of how often—when it all gets to be too much—they just feel like quitting.

9. **Make evaluation procedures transparent.** The students often talked about being confused by the marks they received. They were discouraged by the lack of creativity allowed in response to assignments and they wanted more leeway in deciding how to represent what they were learning. They thought that teachers often felt uncomfortable in the presence of those students who do not easily let them in on who they are, who are enigmas, and who are difficult to reach. Pedagogy is often far from democratic. Teachers tend to promote those who fit in to what they think of as successful. At the crisis point in the play, Sudi Galbeti, a Somalian-Canadian student participant in the production, performed Brian Patten's brilliant poem, "Minister for Exams." (Brian Patten was a famous Liverpool poet who failed his exams and left school at 15. John Patten, his brother, was educated at Wimbledon College and at Cambridge University and later became Britain's Secretary of State for Education in John Major's government from 1992 to 1994.)

Minister for Exams

When I was a child I sat an exam.
The test was so simple
There was no way I could fail.
Q1. Describe the taste of the moon.
It tastes like Creation I wrote; it has the flavour of starlight.
Q2. What colour is Love?
Love is the colour of the water a man lost in the desert finds, I wrote.
Q3. Why do snowflakes melt?
I wrote, they melt because they fall on the warm tongue of God.
There were other questions.
They were as simple.
I described the grief of Adam when he was expelled from Eden.
I wrote down the exact weight of an elephant's dream.
Yet today, many years later, for my living I sweep the streets or clean out the toilets of the fat hotels.
Why? Because constantly I failed my exams.
Why? Well, let me set a test.
Q1. How large is a child's imagination?
Q2. How shallow is the soul of the Minister of Exams?

Brian Patten

10. **We want to succeed.** All of the students recognized that half the battle was finding the motivation within themselves to succeed. In a powerful

scene near the end of the play, students communicated their fervent desire to succeed despite the tremendous difficulties they face. Their honest, authentic voices told of where they had been and where they wanted to go. They talked of the dreams and wishes that their parents had for them and of their desire to make sure they did not disappoint them in any way. One student said that she had been through so much—war, famine, immigration, and prejudice. Even her father did not want her when she was born, she confessed—because he did not believe that girls had any worth. "I will show them all that I can be successful, despite everything," she announced very clearly to the audience. After each student had spoken individually, the group came together, stood in a united formation downstage, and chorally chanted, "WE WILL SUCCEED!"

The cheering and crying during the standing ovation made all of us feel that we had made a profound impression on the audience. In discussions afterwards, we, the company of actors, asked ourselves: "Would the telling of these stories allow the audience to recognize themselves and the truths that were being portrayed? Had audience members been shocked or angered by some of the scenes?" None of us knew for sure. But we all agreed on one fact: to not tell about the suffering of students such as these would be to tell an incomplete story. The students could only tell the stories emanating from their own experiences. Some stories were negative; others were positive. It was up to the audience of educational leaders to sift through these stories, to learn from them, and to act on them.

Potential for Transformation

The experience was transformational for all the participants on many levels. The student actors and their teachers felt proud of their work, in terms of both the performance and the process, and they felt that their voices and experiences had been validated and were ultimately valued. York's teacher candidates came to the realization that they had chosen the right profession, and the theatre students began to think seriously about applying to teacher's college. We will probably never know the full impact of the project on the student actors, but I caught a glimpse of the potential impact in an email from Carole Olsen, the Superintendent of the Halifax School Board. She wrote:

> I know that working with you has created some new defining moments for both our students and staff. They will look back on this experience for the rest of their lives and say, "Remember when…." For one of our students in particular, this opportunity may have transformed her life to the extent that she will choose to remain in high school and graduate. I had the privilege of catching a glimpse of the power of the final production when I observed you working with our students in rehearsal in Halifax. When I spoke to the students on that occasion, I promised them that their voices would be heard and that we would take action on what they told us. I am still committed to following through on that promise.

In fact, the directors and superintendents of education in all three participating boards made arrangements for the students to speak directly to the boards' elected officials and senior staff when the students returned home.

This experience was the highlight of my career as a drama teacher. I have never been more excited to connect with teachers who share the same passions and beliefs that I have about the arts, more honoured to work with a diverse range of talented students, more thrilled to create collective theatre from their authentic voices, or more delighted to be doing difficult and provocative work that matters.

A Teacher's Sense of Students and Students' Sense of Themselves

The students who participated in the "Imagine a School…" project helped me understand many things about teaching and learning in contemporary classrooms. For me, the most powerful learning was this: in order for students to be successful in school, two major things must be in place. One is the teacher's sense of students and the other is the students' sense of themselves. Both need to be in place for harmony to reside in the classroom and for learning to take place. The student actors longed for teachers who understood their backgrounds, identities, learning styles, dreams, and potential. We need teachers, they told us, who have that uncanny sense of knowing what we require at a particular time. They told stories of teachers who had that amazing ability to figure out the best approach for each student—when to push, when to wait, when to challenge, when to comfort, when to create more difficult tasks, when to lay off, when to smile, when to cajole, when to walk away, and when to come back. Teachers' knowledge and skills were important, they told us, but even more important were the relationships that teachers formed with their students based on mutual respect. Education demands alertness, responsiveness, and flexibility from both teachers and students. There need to be relationships established in which conversations about the work that lies ahead is somehow negotiated.

The other key ingredient in teaching fairly is fostering the student's sense of him/herself. Every student needs to experience a sense of place, of honor, and of hope in every classroom in every school. Many of the students in the drama project had begun to lose sight of their dreams. The light and hope that they saw in the eyes of their siblings frightened them because they began to doubt that they could get through school or that they could accomplish anything. They needed teachers to be their cheering section—teachers who continued to believe in them even when they had begun to lose faith in themselves.

For me, the play's key message underlined the indisputable fact that schools need to be places where students can say, "Yes, I am feeling as if I can be successful. I am worth it. I am confident. I am resilient and I can get through this difficult time." Schools must be places where teachers fan the flames of success and optimism and provide guidance, support, understanding, and teaching for everyone. If everyone feels that they have a shot at the future, then tensions between different kinds of students diminishes. Students see that there is room for differences—that we can be individuals, we can come from different parts of the world, and we can enjoy different ways of conducting our lives. And we can all have a shot at the prize—we can all attain our goals. If we are all going to win, we can be more generous with one another and support each other on our journey to success.

Many years ago, Jonothan Neelands, a renowned drama educator from the University of Warwick in England, spoke at a Council of Drama and Dance in Education conference. I think he summed it up best in the words below:

> The self is actually a space of possibles and for many kids…who they think they are is who they have been told they are…and this (definition) is often narrow. "I am shy, I am insecure, I am stupid, I am from the wrong end of town, I cannot be." And often, kids' sense of the possibles of "the other" is also very limited—based on stereotypes that come within the community or from the media—not based on experience at all, but based on what they have been told about "the other." And what we need to do as teachers is to help kids to expand that space of possibles.
>
> So the space of possibles of self include a confident self, a powerful self, a leader self, an achiever self. But at the same time, the space of possibles of "the other" begins to expand so that I understand that those kids who look different from me come in as many different shapes and sizes and forms as I do, or we do. *In that way I can begin to imagine myself as the other and I can begin to imagine the other in myself.* And if we can expand those boundaries out it will be an important way of us feeling comfortable about difference whilst at the same time being able to recognize what is human in each other.

2

What Do We Mean by an Inclusive Curriculum?

I have been fortunate to have spent my professional career in two very different communities. For over 25 years I pursued my teaching career in Toronto—the most mult-iracial, multi-ethnic city in the world. I have worked in elementary and secondary urban classrooms where the challenge to acknowledge and listen to the many voices and expressions of my students confronted me every day. I now find myself living in a rural community in central Ontario where I often teach as a guest in classrooms in small towns in which the racial and ethnic mix of students is not as diverse as in Toronto.

In this rural community, I have worked with students and families confronting a number of socio-economic challenges, especially a lack of access to educational opportunities. I also teach at York University—the third largest university in Canada and one that embraces a large number of students from every country in the world. My students are about as diverse as they can be in terms of race, culture, academic background, class, sexual orientation, and socio-economic status. Every day they teach me about the importance of thinking critically about inclusive curriculum.

The academic, artistic, and social work that takes place in the classroom is dependent on many factors: what the student brings to the classroom in terms of background knowledge, experience, attitudes, and learning style and what the teacher models, expects, wants to happen, knows, values, and provides in terms of resources. So much of the work is dependent on the willingness of teachers to listen to their students, to reflect back to them their identities in the books and resources that they choose, and to find ways to celebrate the diversity within their classrooms in terms of learning style, language, race, sexual orientation, gender, culture, and socio-economic status.

To acknowledge, learn about, and celebrate diversity is a necessary part of curriculum implementation in today's classroom. As difficult and challenging as it is, this work needs to be done if we wish to empower students to understand the issues that have injured people in the past and to help them find their voices so as to change their lives and the world around them in the future. It is important, therefore, to make our classrooms places where students experience equity as part of their daily lives—where they can be part of a community that affirms diversity and promotes intercultural understanding. It is crucial for all of us to co-create classrooms that reflect our students' interests, racial and cultural backgrounds, family relationships, special needs, and unique abilities.

To establish and sustain an inclusive curriculum, we need to:

- find safe and honorable ways to become aware of the varied backgrounds and cultural heritages of our students and to celebrate those differences;
- recognize that our "location" determines what we learn and often how we learn it;
- learn about teaching strategies and resources that will help us build communities of learning in our classrooms in which everyone's voice is heard and valued;
- learn ways to foster inclusive behavior in our schools on the part of both teachers and students;
- demonstrate awareness of the diverse learning styles of our students and teach in a variety of ways to meet varying needs and interests.

Howard Gardner stresses how important this kind of education is in terms of the future success of our students. In his book *Five Minds of the Future* (2006), Gardner describes five sets of cognitive capabilities required by any citizen, professional, or businessperson who desires success. These capabilities include:

- the "disciplined mind": the ability to focus one's mind enough to master a major school of thought such as mathematics, science, or history
- the "synthesizing mind": the ability to integrate diverse ideas into a coherent whole
- the "creating mind": the capacity to uncover new problems and questions, and to solve them
- the "respectful mind": the ability to form and maintain good relationships with other people
- and, finally, the "ethical mind": the ability to fulfill one's responsibilities as a citizen and to identify with other human beings.

For me, an inclusive curriculum incorporates an approach to teaching and learning that recognizes and values the rich diversity of our schools, our students, our communities, and the global population. The goal of an inclusive curriculum is to create a learning environment that reflects, affirms, celebrates, and validates the diversity and complexity of the human experience. Teachers and principals working in inclusive schools approach the curriculum from a multi-faceted perspective, taking into account:

- *what* is taught (content)
- *how* it is taught (pedagogy)
- *two whom* it is taught (access), and
- *under what conditions* it is taught (climate)

Equity Versus Equality

Educators must understand the difference between equity and equality. Equity speaks to differentiated instruction—to teaching and supporting students in ways that will allow them to benefit from equal opportunities. Equality means that we strive to teach everyone exactly the same curriculum. However, this approach cannot work when we know that we have to help those students who did not come into our classrooms from the same starting point. We have to help students in different ways by teaching them with a fair and just outcome in mind.

An Inclusive and Equitable School Environment

I had the opportunity to teach a three-year Additional Qualifications course (described later in the book) with a group of anti-racist educators: teachers, principals, vice-principals, and consultants. As we worked together during the course, we got to know each other well and we spent a lot of time discussing the classrooms in which we taught. During the time that we spent together, the participants in the course changed schools, grades, subjects, and responsibilities. Over time, we began to develop a way to describe what an inclusive, equitable school environment should look like, sound like, and feel like for everyone. We used our imaginations to enter various kinds of rooms in the schools in which we taught and we asked ourselves critical questions about the appearance, content, use, and access associated with those rooms. Here are some of the questions we created together:

HALLWAYS

1. Are the signs, notices, posters, motivational comments, and displays in the school building multilingual, and do they reflect a variety of cultural perspectives?
2. Are students' home languages used in school announcements?
3. Is there a private place where students can pray if they wish to?
4. Are the hall monitors seen as part of the school staff? Are they invited to staff meetings and offered appropriate professional development?
5. Are teachers present in the hallways during breaks?
6. Is material that is on display representative of different cultural and racial groups?

SCHOOL LIBRARY

1. Is the library open after school so that students who do not have access to computers and the Internet at home can do their homework and research?
2. Is there a wide range of materials that reflect the diverse population in the school?
3. What kinds of activities are the students engaged in?
4. Is there a system in place for students to get the help that they need?
5. Are students allowed to talk and interact as long as they do not disturb others?
6. Are there breakout rooms for student meetings?

CAFETERIA

1. Is there a wide variety of food available that reflect students' cultures?
2. Are there enough chairs for all students to sit and eat?
3. Are there enough garbage cans and recyclable bins so that the tables can be cleaned up quickly?
4. What kind of music is playing? Does the kind of music change regularly?

SCHOOL OFFICE

1. Are translation services available for parents who do not speak English?
2. How long do visitors have to wait before they are looked after?
3. Are students treated with the same respect as visitors, parents/guardians, and teachers?

Besides imagining the physical attributes of the rooms in the school, we also looked at the inclusiveness of school activities, the varying attitudes of people in the school and their relationships to each other and to the students, and finally, the conversations that took place amongst and between individuals and groups. We focused as well on the conversations that happened in the classroom, the kinds of activities that were included in the curriculum, and the amount of engagement on the part of the students. We asked ourselves how special events, extra-curricular programs, and community and parental involvement could be re-envisioned and made more inclusive.

In terms of curriculum, the Equity Studies Department encouraged us to move beyond the "heroes and heroine curriculum" (as described in James A. Banks's *Multicultural Education: Historical Development, Dimensions, and Practice*) to one that was relatively more transformational and critical. The Equity Studies Department has since developed an observation checklist for teachers who want to be more inclusive in their practice. I have adapted it as shown in the blackline master that appears on pages 146–148 at the back of this book.

I encourage my student teachers to ask themselves, "What do I want my classroom to feel like, look like, and sound like? What overriding quality do I want to establish from the beginning of the year until the end? How will I get each one of my students to sparkle in her or his own personal way? How will I nurture, support, inspire, and challenge them to take risks so they will think critically about the things they are learning and communicate their new knowledge to me and to others in exciting ways?"

All teachers want the community of students in their classrooms to feel that they are individually as well as collectively valued. Teachers want their classrooms to be places where there is not just tolerance but respect; where there is not just group process but community; where there are relationships and not just connections; and where there is empathy and compassion based on understanding rather than superficial encounters. To help them build this kind of community, I encourage teachers to find their own guiding metaphors. Over the years, teachers become attached to various metaphors that help them establish their vision for the work and relationships that will develop in their classrooms so they can pursue teaching in a reflective way. In my work with pre-service teachers at York University's Faculty of Education, one of my student teachers, Jon Annis, envisioned his classroom as a "Clave Classroom," which he describes thus:

> At the heart of most Afro-Cuban rhythms is the clave pattern. A clave is a constant two-bar rhythmic pattern with specific positioning of the accents that repeat throughout a song. It is the foundation for Cuban rhythms and is the constant underpinning that any musician in the ensemble can hear if he or she becomes lost. The clave will be the foundation of my classrooms. It will represent the consistent strength of community inside the room. Its repeating pattern signifies what my students can expect every time they walk through the door. They will encounter a safe environment that guides them back on

track when we get lost, one that holds us together while others catch up, and one that doesn't judge others on where they came from or where they are going. The clave is not always heard as musicians often feel its sensations even in its absence.

The Importance of Courageous Leadership

Andy Hargreaves, Thomas More Brennan Chair in the Lynch School of Education at Boston College, reminds us that teachers are leaders of young people and that leading and teaching are interconnected. In *The Seven Principles of Sustainable Leadership* (2003), Hargreaves and his co-author Dean Fink (of the International Centre for Educational Change at the Ontario Institute for Studies in Education at the University of Toronto) explain:

> Sustainable leadership matters, spreads and lasts. It is a shared responsibility, that does not unduly deplete human or financial resources, and that cares for and avoids exerting negative damage on the surrounding educational and community environment. Sustainable leadership has an activist engagement with the forces that affect it, and builds an educational environment of organizational diversity that promotes cross-fertilization of good ideas and successful practices in communities of shared learning and development.

In my experience, successful inclusive schools evolve when courageous leadership is in place, when teachers collaborate with each other, when the principal values everyone's work and does not play favorites, when leadership is shared, when students' identities are explicit and honored, when all students are seen as an investment rather than a cost, and when everyone has a vision and a belief in a future filled with high expectations for all learners.

When I was a very young teacher—in my third year of teaching—a new principal arrived at my high school. Bob Brooks was a dynamic leader who advanced many exciting ideas. Unfortunately, he died suddenly over the mid-year holidays and we returned to a school without a principal. For some reason, the board of education did not replace Bob until the following September. Therefore, from January until June, the staff pitched in to keep the school functioning at the high academic level for which it was known. The heads of departments shared the leadership and the school functioned very well. I witnessed well-organized and respectful staff meetings in which the staff was consulted and their input valued. I watched teachers who had been on the sidelines come forth to make significant contributions by serving on committees to enact changes in the way that things had been done in the school for years. I was amazed at how exciting it was to teach in a large, urban collegiate setting in which everyone's voice mattered.

Collegiality, Collaboration, and Mentorship

In *Improving Schools from Within: Teachers, Parents and Principals Can Make the Difference* (1990), Roland S. Barth reminds us that collegiality is signaled by the presence of four behaviors, as outlined on the following page.

Courage is not limited to the battlefield or to the Indianapolis 500 or bravely catching a thief in your house. The real tests of courage are...the inner tests, like remaining faithful when nobody's looking, like enduring pain when the room is empty, like standing alone when you're misunderstood, like fighting for what is right even when you know you are going to lose.

Charles R. Swindoll

- Adults in school talk about practice; these conversations are frequent, continuous, concrete, and precise.
- Adults in schools observe each other engaged in the practice of teaching and administration.
- Adults engage in work on curriculum, by planning, designing, researching, and evaluating curriculum.
- Finally, adults in schools teach each other what they know about teaching, learning, assessing, and leading. Knowledge of the art and craft of teaching is revealed, articulated, and shared.

In order to do the kind of work demanded by social justice education, attention must be paid to the kinds of relationships among the adults in the school. The kind of leadership that develops must allow for important and courageous conversations to take place about fair and decent practice so that teachers can then move into the realm of critical theorizing about their teaching.

This means that principals must be brave and encourage their staffs to talk about topics that might make some teachers uncomfortable. It is important to understand and articulate honestly how we view ourselves, our students, and our classrooms. This openness can make us fearful of being judged, speculated about, and scrutinized. But in order for teachers to teach fairly, they need to be aware of how they and their students live within the context of their school, their community, and the larger society. The conversations can be awkward at first, but they allow teachers to begin to re-evaluate their belief systems around questions of identity, racism, classism, ageism, and sexual orientation, amongst others.

In most schools, mentorship programs have been established. These programs are monitored by trusted "outsiders" (such as board consultants, educational leaders, and instructional leaders) who ask mentors to be honest when they answer questions such as:

- Do I offer my students and my peers challenging ideas?
- Do I set challenges for myself?
- Am I helping to build self-confidence and independence on the part of my students and my peers?
- Am I offering constructive criticism?
- Am I encouraging good teaching?
- Am I encouraging professional behavior?
- Am I teaching by example?

It seems to me that in inclusive schools, the questions that teachers ask themselves go even further: such questions move teachers beyond what they take for granted and what they currently understand. Here are some questions that mentors might help teachers ask themselves:

- Am I aware of my subjectivities when I teach?
- Do I understand the attitudes, needs, behaviors, dreams, and aspirations of the students whom I teach?
- Do I defer judgement until I get to know my students?
- Do I welcome discovery and surprise in my teaching?
- Do I monitor myself for bias and discrimination in terms of my role as teacher, as well as in terms of my perceptions of the students whom I teach?
- Do I have preconceived ideas about the community in which I teach?

We cannot handle the dilemmas and the crises and the evil of these times alone. And so we are at a point when our very negative images of one another, and when the glorification of the individual, the hero, the individual savior, are part of the problem. I believe that the single most important act and gesture of our times, given how dark and cold we are, is coming back together.

Margaret Wheatley

- Do I work towards significance in my teaching?
- Is my teaching interactive?
- Do I tap into my students' personal experiences?
- Do I provide time for my students to share different insights into what they are learning?
- Do I help students understand how they will be evaluated?

Pat Mora, an American writer and teacher who has championed anti-discriminatory teaching for many years, asks the following key questions to help teachers in their journey toward establishing inclusive classrooms:

1. Do I play an active role in creating an inclusive school community, a community in which each person is valued?
2. Have I assessed my own heritage? Have I assessed the assumptions and values that emerge from my personal history?
3. Have I assessed the cultural backgrounds of my students? Have I acknowledged the need to continue learning about our human diversity and the need to honor the cultures, languages, and family backgrounds of my students?
4. Do I encourage participation by all parents/family members in the educational experiences of their children, including non-English-speaking parents and parents with limited economic means?
5. Do I avoid defining culture only in terms of food, folklore, fashion, and festivals?
6. Do I create a classroom climate in which no culture dominates, in which all languages are valued, and in which all learning styles are encouraged?
7. Does my classroom/library/school reflect equally the contributions of our country's many heritages?
8. Do I provide varied reading and writing experiences that reflect local, regional, and national diversity?
9. Do I select diverse curriculum materials on the basis of authenticity and do these materials reflect cultural complexities rather than reinforce stereotypes?
10. Does my classroom/library/school prepare students to participate actively in a pluralistic society?

Imagining Yourself Forward

"Imagining yourself forward" is another effective approach that teachers can adopt to sustain an inclusive curriculum. Look closely at who you are and what you wish to accomplish—and then imagine yourself forward to the kind of teacher that you want to be in the future.

As I mentioned earlier, I teach in the pre-service program at the Faculty of Education at York University. When my students come back to class after their first block of practice teaching in November, some of them are quite discouraged. They are overwhelmed by the complexity of teaching. Some feel that they might not be able to be successful at teaching because they realize they have so much to learn. To help offset their discouragement, I ask them to "imagine themselves forward" and to write their retirement speeches. I ask them to imagine that thirty years have passed and that a party has been organized to honor their achievements as a teacher who has made a difference in the lives of their students. They write about what they learned, what they did, and what they wished they had done. Here is an excerpt from one of my students' reflections:

First, I'd like to thank all of you for braving the fierce storm we're having tonight to be here at what marks the end of my career in teaching. Now if the group in the corner wouldn't mind backing away from the pork roast for just a few minutes, I'll begin…. Before beginning my teaching career I remember hearing the stories. Mainly the stories told of new teachers who at first were naïve and idealistic in their teaching ambitions—that is, until they actually began to teach. After encountering a dose of real-life classroom experience, they soon became wise to the "reality" of teaching. Within this reality, teachers became jaded and cynical and ultimately complacent about their "jobs." That was my greatest fear upon entering the teaching profession—that I would cease to care and, even more so, that I would cease to care that I didn't care.

I remember the key teachers throughout my life: Grade 6—the teacher who expected more from me because he believed that I was capable of meeting his higher standards. Secondary school—the teacher whose passion for teaching was fueled by his talent and love of music. University—the professor who showed unconditional support and faith in my success despite the challenges encountered throughout my learning process. These teachers were pivotal in helping me define not only who I was at various points in my learning but also who I wanted to become as I continued along my path as both a student and an educator.

In the initial stage of my journey, during my first teaching block, a shift occurred in my thinking about teaching. First, I was confronted by the fact that teaching was more complicated than I'd ever anticipated. Factors such as classroom management, timing, accommodations, and the curriculum were suddenly thrown into my act as I struggled to "perform' my teacherly role. It also dawned on me that this endeavor was no "act"—or if it was, it was one which required a lot of improvisation as the unexpected came into play.

My other realization was that my thoughts regarding the student-teacher dynamic, which I had formulated mainly as a student, were not completely accurate. The relationship was not as one-sided as I'd assumed, but instead was a symbiotic one. I came to this knowledge as I learned from my students every day, including, more often than not, what not to do again. It was within this first teaching block then that I also came to understand my journey would involve a continual process of both learning and teaching.

In this way, I came to view the classroom as an environment which was constantly shifting and in flux in order to meet the highly individualized needs and demands of its various parts. I learned to be flexible, to never make assumptions. I also learned that in order to be an effective educator, one must simultaneously play both the role of the educator and the learner, and most importantly, that sometimes the best way to change a system is to work from within.

Well, it looks like the dessert table is almost ready for you, so on a final note, thank you, everyone, for the lovely encyclopedia set and Chia Pet. I will cherish them always.

Raffaela

The challenges in teaching posed by limited time, resources, energy, creative ideas, and group process skills are enormous. To overlay goals of social justice and inclusive education seems to intensify the pressure. Here is my advice. Start from where you are. Begin with your core beliefs and then modify them as you experience the world of teaching and learning. Be open to the array of experiences represented by the human beings in your classrooms whom you are getting to know. Find out about your students—learn their names and how they got them; learn about what they do after school; what their families are like. What is their lived experience and how does it impact on what it is you are going to teach them? What do your students already know that you do not? How can your worlds coalesce so that you can establish a relationship based on genuine interest in one another? It *is* important to look beyond one's self and to reach out to the student who needs to learn in different ways. Examine critically the things you are trying to do with your students and be ready to rethink your strategies, techniques, and interventions so that you do not get stuck teaching something that is not appropriate for the kinds of learners with whom you interact each day. It is vitally important to look beyond teaching plans to find out where your students are from so that you can continue the learning journey together:

> Good teachers join self, subject, and students into the fabric of life because they teach from an integral and undivided self; they manifest in their own lives and evoke in their students a "capacity for connectedness." They are able to weave a complex web of connections between themselves, their subjects, and their students, so that students can learn to weave a world of connections for themselves. The methods used by these weavers vary widely: lectures, Socratic dialogues, laboratory experiments, collaborative problem solving, creative chaos. The connections made by good teachers are sustained not in their methods but in their hearts. In this context, "heart" is meant in its ancient sense: the place where intellect and emotion and spirit and will converge in the human self.
>
> Patrick Palmer

3

Building Community

I entered the classroom with the conviction that it was crucial for me and every other student to be an active participant, not a passive consumer.... education as the practice of freedom.... education that connects the will to know with the will to become. Learning is a place where paradise can be created.

bell hooks

When I taught in a downtown Toronto high school, I would ask my students to take me on a walk to places in their community that they felt I needed to know about. The students worked in groups and planned several community walks. Parks, corner store hangouts, restaurants, and community centers were always on the list. One day I went to a pool hall to meet the manager. Another time, I was taken to the beach. Many of my students worked at a Bingo Palace that was close to my home. I had never played Bingo but I remember the excited look on the face of Tyrone, one of my students, when my husband and I entered and sat down to play. Tyrone proudly brought us each a soft drink and welcomed us to his workplace. This visit made a difference in my relationship with Tyrone and in the level of success that he subsequently attained in my classroom.

Patrick Solomon, a past colleague of mine in the Faculty of Education at York University, encouraged student teachers at York to take several walks in the community surrounding the school in which they are about to teach. He encouraged the student teachers to pay attention to details—and to ask questions to get to know the community that feeds the school both literally and figuratively. In his book, *Urban Teacher Education and Teaching: Innovative Practices for Diversity and Social Justice* (2007), he posed questions such are these:

1. How do we provide adequate learning experiences so as to give voices to the most vulnerable in urban, inner city environments: those who are socially different by virtue of race and ethnicity, social class and poverty location, immigrant status and language status?
2. What awareness, skills, and sensibilities do we need in order to critically analyze the link between the structural impediments of urban inner-city communities and those of the schools located within them, to challenge the ideological positioning that both gives rise to and sustains reproductive pedagogical practices in urban schools?
3. How do we begin to utilize the historically subjugated community knowledge and resources as authentic curriculum content?
4. How do we establish authentic democratic educational partnerships with the communities served by the school (e.g., parents, families, social and cultural organizations) in order to develop their social and cultural capital?

5. How do we attract and retain teachers with high-level skills for success in urban settings, respond to the struggle for teacher professionalism, and provide environments for practitioners to grow on the job?
6. How do we rise about the rigid hierarchical structures and bureaucracies that paralyze innovative professional ideas and activities in urban settings, so as to develop the political skills and courage to fight resistance to change and engage in transformational work in urban communities?

Creating Community: Moving Beyond Estrangement and Alienation

The associate dean of the Faculty of Education at York University, Don Dippo, is interested in what happens when communities and schools coalesce. Don was a guest speaker at a seminar course that I developed for 16 teachers in the Toronto District School Board Willow Park cluster of schools. The course was called "Conversations About Community Engagement: Sharing the Stories, Mapping Our Understandings, Teaching With New Eyes." What would happen, Don wondered aloud, if a school held its staff meeting in the local mall? The teachers could buy their coffees and donuts from the coffee shop, and after the meeting they could wander through the mall and do some errands. Think about 120 teachers sitting in a mall talking about the students who live, study, and work in the community. Consider the "optics" of this scenario. The teachers and administrators would be perceived as visibly supporting the community as a part of it rather than as separate from it. Psychological and social barriers would come tumbling down; teachers would be viewed as members of the community rather than as people who drop in to teach and then leave for their homes in more middle-class neighborhoods.

What other school-community interactions might schools undertake? One possibility would be to hold a staff meeting in a community room in an apartment building near the school. A community organization or a restaurant could provide refreshments. Perhaps a teacher could supervise high school students or college students who live in apartment buildings as they run a homework club. If parents or guardians cannot be at home after school to supervise their children, this circumstance could offer another opportunity for community involvement. For example, I am a member of the Jane-Finch artist community council that designs after-school and co-curricular events for students and their families in the community surrounding York University. The artists live and work in the community and enrich the lives of the students by their art and by their commitment to making connections with them.

New Beginnings: I See…, I Wonder…, I Hope…

The first few days of school are exciting. These days usher in a sense of hope. It's a time for students to open fresh notebooks and begin to write a whole new page of their lives. It is also a time that brings sleepless nights as students and teachers readjust to the routines and rhythms of school life. It takes effort to put away the days of summer—to pack up our summer memories and head into tighter schedules, heavier responsibilities, and more demanding mental work. That first day, everyone has mixed emotions—anticipation interwoven with anxiety. I joke with my colleagues that the feelings of dread dissipate as I stand by the photocopying machine. The beginning has happened—there is nothing more that I can do—and in a few minutes all eyes will be on me!

On that first day of school, I always wonder: "*If I am feeling so much worry, how are my students feeling?*" If, so far, they have done well in school, I know that they will enter my classroom more confidently than those who have struggled to pass tests, to get along with others, and to feel included. For those students who find "doing" school challenging, I ask myself all sorts of questions: What are their expectations? How fearful are they? How will established school patterns have affected their behavior? With whom will they surround themselves in order to feel safe?

I wonder how the students will enter my classroom. Will they be propelled by a desire to make it right this time and avoid becoming snared by the discouragement and disenchantment of past failures? Or, will they enter with bravado, wearing bold masks of power to hide their vulnerability? Will they reach out to me—or pretend that they do not care?

I also wonder how I will react to my students on that first day. *Can I find a way to extend my hand so that I can nurture them and we can all move forward?* Instinctively, I know that I will have to wait to get answers to all of these questions, and when I do, the answers will not be definitive, but tentative. I will have to teach and wait and watch in order to know how to proceed.

All of us are intent on establishing and nurturing positive classroom relationships. We also want to harness creativity and set engaging contexts in which students can speak, read, and write with real purpose. But many of us have students who block that work and make teaching and learning problematic and sometimes even impossible. One student's negative behavior can alter the entire classroom dynamic. *What do we do about the students who challenge us and make life problematic?*

I encourage teachers to talk to each other about these students. It is not shameful to not how to cope with challenging students. Our colleagues possess a wealth of knowledge and experience. They can help and support us. When private questions are aired in public forums—such as staff meetings and professional development seminars—further questions and discussion result. Usually, the questions invite collective critical thinking and interaction that lead to important rethinking of teaching practice.

In workshops, I often ask teachers to think about the student who is most on their minds. Perhaps a student is disruptive in class or is unable to function in small groups. Perhaps a student has just arrived from another school or from another country. Perhaps a student is so shy and quiet that she or he is often overlooked. I ask the workshop participants to imagine what these students are thinking and feeling as they sit in their classrooms. Teachers smile wanly as I ask them to focus on that one student. Often, the sessions I conduct are at the end of a long teaching day. Revisiting classrooms in their imaginations takes effort.

To begin the exercise, I ask teachers to record three phrases on a large index card:

I see ...

I wonder...

I hope...

Next, I ask the teachers to write about the student for ten minutes. At a seminar course that I conducted in the Toronto District School Board, Cyril Lewin, one of the teachers, wrote:

I see…
this young man saunter into the classroom, oblivious of everyone else, eyes downcast as he meanders between his classmates and the furniture in his quest for his sanctuary, his chair. Hands deeply immersed in his pockets, his chair strategically away from his desk and from other members of his group, he ignores everyone and everything around him.

I wonder…
if he will one day actively participate and end his seclusion. Will he accept his new environment, new classmates, new routines?

I hope…
that he transforms sooner, rather than later. I hope that I discover the strategy to break down his barriers and that I will see him full of motivation, energy and mirth.

In partners, we read our cards aloud. Then, as a group, we share our imaginings. Some of us cry with frustration; some of us laugh in recognition as difficult teaching encounters are described. All of us support one another as we try to figure out how to help these students who keep us awake at night.

I am always moved by these discussions—by teachers' strong desire to find ways of reaching their students by trying a new strategy, discarding an approach that has not worked, or rethinking the reason they are doing what they are doing. I am always impressed by teachers' willingness to change direction to benefit their students and by their perseverance in the face of curriculum overload, time constraints, and many other pressures.

The Six Es of Effective Teaching

I have discovered a way to be mindful of what kinds of opportunities and supports I want to offer all of my students. I have done so by developing a framework that allows me to establish compassionate learning communities, honor students as individuals, celebrate collective achievement, and help students value and love learning. My work is anchored in what I call the "Six Es of Effective Teaching":

- Keep **E**xpectations high.
- Establish an inclusive, respectful **E**nvironment for learning.
- **E**ngage the learner.
- **E**xplore learning actively.
- **E**xtend the learning.
- **E**valuate fairly in an unfair world.

The rest of this chapter discusses the first two Es of Effective Teaching. Chapters 4 and 5 explore the remaining four Es in the context of active engagement with rich source material designed to stimulate critical thinking and emotional literacy.

Keep Expectations High

It is up to all of us to make classrooms places where students want to be, where they see themselves as capable of success, and where they can "imagine themselves forward." As I stated previously, I believe that all students wish to be privately happy and publicly useful and that most of them realize that education is the ticket to their success. I must, however, pay particular attention to those students who have difficulty believing that they are ever going to succeed.

The first few weeks of any academic year or semester are crucial in establishing the expectations and routines that will govern students' chances of success. The relationships built between students and teachers make a huge difference. I plan for those moments as much as I plan my lessons. I think about how to greet my students and where to stand each morning. Usually, I stand in the hallway and welcome my students into the classroom. I make sure I say "Hello" and "Welcome back!" to everyone—not just to the students I have met or taught previously. I can usually tell who is feeling confident and who is feeling frightened and insecure, but I try not to form quick opinions.

When we meet our students on that first day of classes, we enter into a relationship—into a formal contract—in which rules are negotiated, routines are set, and respect is established. With each passing day, we define the contract further: differences are recognized, helpful feedback is offered, identities are honored, diverse learning needs are identified, inventive strategies are implemented, and success is monitored. The students are assessing you as much as you are assessing them. Will you be fair, kind, and non-judgemental? Can you be trusted?

I maintain high expectations for all my students, *doing my best* to *withhold judgement about them*—academically and socially—for as long as I can. I expect my students to do well. I set the bar high and if necessary, adjust teaching strategies to make sure students reach that height. It is up to me and up to them, and usually we can work together to find ways to make success happen.

Some of our students have lost faith in themselves and in the school system by the time they come into our lives. They do not hold out much hope for their future. Schools and teachers need to be there for these students. We need to realize that the contracts that we negotiate together not only affect the teaching and learning climate for the next ten months, but these understandings can influence how our students regard themselves as learners and citizens for many years to come. We need to think of learning as something connected to creativity, responsibility, innovation, and enterprise.

Establish an Inclusive, Respectful Environment for Learning

It is important to establish an ethic whereby everyone listens to each person's individual voice in the classroom. For this to happen, students need to know that they can count on intellectual, social, physical, and emotional support from the teacher *and* from their peers. As students are challenged to take risks in their learning—to speak in class, to read aloud, to write, and to engage in group work—they need to understand that everyone in the class is rooting for them, that they are part of a community that respects and supports them, and that they can feel safe. This confidence to take risks will come only if relationships in the classroom are based on mutual respect.

Rules of Engagement

At the beginning of the year, therefore, I spend time building relationships among my students. This cultivation of respect is not only my responsibility, but also my students': everyone contributes to building a positive classroom community. Students need opportunities to engage in group-building activities that will let them get to know one another not only superficially, but in ways that make them think about others, empathize with them, and celebrate everyone's achievements.

As they learn about one another, students grow conscious of how their individual behavior affects everyone in their presence. What might they learn to do, say, and change about their behavior to improve the classroom dynamic? We talk about how all of us need to learn to manage our emotions, develop self-awareness, and remain alert to how our emotions and reactions play out in the classroom. The real work lies in helping students behave as responsible individuals who can act in their own interest while weighing the rights and interests of others at the same time. This learning related to character development is as important as academic achievement.

Respect runs two ways. An acceptance of the importance of teamwork is needed to create an inclusive classroom environment. Students must come to understand that negotiation is part of learning and working together, and that everyone should have a voice in what happens in school. I foster collaboration among my students and work hard and thoughtfully to diminish competition. I never reward groups with prizes, candy, fake money, or food—completing the task to everyone's satisfaction is reward enough.

I try to maintain a balance of control and autonomy. I tell them that I am working towards fairness and, if I make a mistake (and I will), I will apologize. I collaborate with students to negotiate the rules of engagement in the classroom. They all learn pretty quickly that I need to have silence when I speak and give directions, so I let them know that this is one of my key rules. Over the years, the rules change, but here are some that students have felt very strongly about:

1. Information that we share as a class stays within the class.
2. Try to think of others as you think about yourself.
3. Think before you speak.
4. Don't let one or two people dominate class discussions.
5. Seek out the opinions of the shy people but don't put them on the spot.
6. Allow us the right to pass.
7. No name-calling.
8. No tricks on tests.
9. No food rewards/prizes.
10. Everyone should look after the classroom space.

Something I have learned over the years is that providing positive, collective feedback at regular intervals is a powerful motivational strategy. This kind of feedback is genuine and works much better than singling out students for doing something right or wrong, as in "I like how Ahmed is completing his work." My recommended approach is not competitive, does not play students off against each other, and does not generate envy or distrust. I stay tuned to positive moments and give immediate collective praise and feedback to the whole class. Doing so helps spur the entire group to work more effectively and efficiently with one another. The results can be astonishing.

Because I want to get to know my students in terms of who they are and what they hope school will bring to them, I ask them to fill out the self-assessment form on the facing page at the beginning of the academic year.

Establish a Respectful Environment Through Cooperative Games

At the beginning of the school year, cooperative games provide an enjoyable way for students to learn each other's names and to relax with each other by laughing and having fun. These games help students get to know one another by encouraging them to interact with as many people as possible in the class. These games also encourage students' listening and observation skills as they build self-esteem. Students enjoy opportunities to talk about their positive traits, to give feedback to each other, and to monitor their feelings and responses. As students get to know one another, the games can be adapted and used for other learning purposes. By participating in these games, students can begin to look more critically at human interactions and to talk about their intellectual and emotional responses to these interactions in an honest and open fashion. If you structure cooperative games carefully, a great deal of trust and mutual appreciation can grow amongst students and their classmates.

At first, I start off with fun, interactive games that are easy to learn. I have students play them quickly so that any embarrassment is diminished. I make sure that students are caught up in a whirlwind of activity. Here are a few of the games that students have enjoyed playing as a way to "break the ice" at the beginning of a school year or semester:

Say Hello

Have the students stand in a circle. Have each student say their name and perform an action. Have the other students repeat the name and the action. Continue around the circle until everyone has had a turn. Tell the students that they do not have to plan the action but rather they should try to do it as spontaneously as possible.

Play the game again, but vary it. Have individual students say their names and perform an action that is squiggly, straight, robot-like, exaggerated, and so on. Then have them say their names loudly, in a whisper, in a singsong voice, or in whatever way they wish. The rest of the class mimics the qualities of the physical action or the vocal twist while saying each person's name.

Next, have students say "hello" in their own languages. Have them stand in a circle. They say their greeting and the rest of the class repeats it. If the student's home language is English, they can say hello in different ways, for example, *hi; howya doing?; hey, there*. The important point is to have the rest of the class repeat the greeting. Students can help each other with pronunciation. The rest of the class can guess what the language is or the student can share that information with the group before he or she teaches the word for "hello."

Imagining and Hoping

I am (age, grade) _____

I am interested in finding out about _____

_____

Some people consider me _____

I think of myself as _____

I want to be considered (*check off any of the adjectives in the list below*):

STEADFAST	❑	CREATIVE	❑
RESILIENT	❑	NURTURING	❑
LOYAL	❑	STRONG	❑
ETHICAL	❑	COURAGEOUS	❑
USEFUL	❑	ACTIVE	❑
ACCOUNTABLE	❑	FAIR	❑
CARING	❑	DETERMINED	❑
PATIENT	❑	OPEN	❑
PROUD	❑		

To become the person I want to be, I need to do the following:

_____

_____

_____

_____

_____

Some of the roadblocks that might make my progress difficult are:

_____

_____

_____

_____

_____

_____

Atom

Have students "walk to the empty spaces in the room" without bumping into one another. Have them walk quickly, change direction, walk on tiptoes, walk backwards, walk sideways, and so on. On a signal such as a tambourine tap or a drumbeat, have them freeze. Congratulate them and then tell them to relax. Advise them that they are going to repeat the activity but this time when you say, "Atom 3!" they are going to behave as if they are atoms and join up with the students who are closest to them to form a group of three. They are to quickly learn each other's names. Then they are to walk throughout the room again as individuals. If you say, "Atom 5!," they are to form a group of five. If anyone is left over, students are to hide those people in the group constellation. Circulate around the classroom and check to find the extra people hidden in the group. Keep the groups moving and changing until everyone has been jumbled up and can name five new classmates' names.

Birthday Line

Have the students arrange themselves in two equal groups facing each other in a straight line. One line is Team X and the other is Team Y. Each team is to work together without talking, as quickly as they can. On your signal, have students arrange themselves in the order of their birthday months. Have the students say their birthday out loud and as they do so, ask all of the students to pay attention. After this part of the game, ask students if they heard any birthdays to which they can make a personal connection, for example, "My sister has the same birthday as Janet. Rashid and I have the same birthday and we never even knew that all last year!" Finally, have the students line up in alphabetical order according to their first names. Have them say their name out loud so that everyone can hear each name and the correct pronunciation. (When I do workshops in schools, this game gives me an opportunity to hear how students want their names pronounced. I have them play the game every time I visit. I take special care not to mispronounce names and thus I avoid embarrassing students.)

Back to Back/Face to Face

Have students find a partner and stand back to back just far enough away not to be touching each other. Have them change their position as you call out different commands such as "Face to Face," "Side to Side," "Shoulder to Shoulder," "Elbow to Elbow," "Elbow to Shoulder," and so on. When you say "Change partners," students find another partner and the commands begin again. Encourage students to find as many partners as possible and to learn their names in the split second of meeting each person!

The Seat on My Right Is Free

Students sit on chairs in a circle. Make sure that there is one empty chair. The person to the left of the chair says, "The seat on my right is free. I would like to invite [someone in the class] to sit beside me." The person who is invited crosses the circle, which frees up a chair. The game continues as the person to the left of the empty chair repeats, "The seat on my right is free. I would like [name of classmate] to sit beside me." Establish the rule that everyone should receive an invitation and that no person can be invited more than once.

Name Switch Now

Students stand in a circle. One person volunteers to be "It." "It" establishes eye contact with someone across the circle. "It" then says his/her name and the name of the person with whom he/she has made eye contact. "It" begins to walk toward this person. This individual establishes eye contact with another person, says his/her name along with the name of the first person, and begins walking toward him or her. They switch places. The game should be played quickly and everyone should have a turn.

Heigh Ho!

Students sit on chairs in a circle. Appoint someone to be "It." "It" stands in the middle of the circle and says, "Everyone who is wearing sandals change places." Everyone wearing sandals moves to another chair. "It" goes to a chair and sits down. This will leave someone standing; that person becomes "It." "It"" then says, for example, "Everyone who watched TV last night, change places." or "Everyone who wishes it was still summer vacation, change places." If the person who is "It" says, "Heigh Ho!," everyone must change places. Play the game quickly.

Sushi

Students sit on chairs in a circle. Brainstorm a list of ingredients for sushi (for example, rice, fish, ginger, seaweed, soya sauce) and write them on the board. Go around the circle and assign each student an ingredient. Have someone stand in the center of the circle as "It." "It" calls out an ingredient. All the rice people have to change seats. The person left over is "It." The person can call out "Rice" and "Soya Sauce" and those people have to change seats. Alternatively, "It" can call out "Sushi" and everyone has to change places. You can alter the game to include favorite recipes from around the world: taboulleh, lentil soup, perogis, hamburgers, and so on.

Games that Focus on Equity and Inclusion

Here are some games that can be adapted for other purposes (described in the summary of each game below):

Concentric Circles

This game encourages student to share information about themselves at the beginning of the school year. You can also play it again throughout the year to elicit responses to what is being discussed in class. As the students get to know each other better, you can play this game so that they begin to think about and discuss the ways in which inequality and discrimination have affected them, members of their families, or people whom they have met or read about.

Have the students find a partner and decide who is A and who is B. Have the Bs move their chairs into an area of the classroom and form a circle facing out. The As then move their chairs to an outer circle, facing in. In this way, the As are facing the Bs. Tell the students that you are going to give them a question to exchange with their partners. The As have less than one minute to respond to Bs' question. Then the Bs will have less than one minute to respond to the same question. Provide a signal such as a drumbeat when you want the conversation to stop. When the drumbeat sounds for the second time, the As stand up and move to sit on a chair to the right. The inner circle remains stationary so that each person has a new partner. A new question is then posed. Continue having the students in the outer circle rotate to face new partners as many times as possible.

When I play this game with a new group of students, I make sure that the questions I pose are non-threatening. Here are some examples:

- What do you like to do in your spare time?
- How many brothers and sisters do you have? Describe their characteristics.
- If you could have one wish granted, what would it be?

As I get to know the class better, I create different prompts for the conversations and I give students more time to respond to one another:

- Describe a time in your life when you didn't get what you wanted.
- Describe a difficult decision that you had to make in your life or tell about a time when a difficult decision was made on your behalf.
- Describe the person in your life whom you admire the most. Why do you admire this person?

Sometimes you can brainstorm various kinds of conversational prompts with the class before you play the game, for example:

- Tell your partner about a time when you were treated unfairly by someone.
- If you could change the world in one way, what would you do?
- If you could turn back time, what choice or choices would you make differently?

You can play this game as you work with different source material (see Chapters 4 and 5 in this book). Here are some examples:

- What do you think Elsewhere is like? (*The Giver*)
- Do you think that Walter and Ruth have a good marriage? Why or why not? (*A Raisin in the Sun*)
- Why do you think Lucia stayed in the village for as long as she did? What was she hoping to accomplish? (*The Woman Who Outshone the Sun*)
- Have you ever known anyone who was treated unfairly as Merrick was because of a physical deformity? (*The Elephant Man*)

Concentric Circles in Role

You can adapt the previous game into a role-playing exercise. The As play the role of a reporter who is trying to find out information about the characters, relationships, and events depicted in the literature you are teaching. The Bs play the role of a character in the story or poem.

- A: Reporter; B: Shopkeeper. Question: Had the boy ever been into your store in the past? ("The Man who Discovers That His Son Has Become a Thief")
- A: Reporter; B: Priest. Question: What would the church's views be on the way that the villagers are treating the stranger who has come to the island? (*The Island*)

- A: Reporter. B: Merrick's father. Question: Were you aware of how your new wife felt about your son? Did you do anything to stop the abuse? (*The Elephant Man*)

Who Are We? Where Are We?

Have the class push the desks and chairs back so that there is a large space in the classroom. Ask for a volunteer to think of a place where a large number of people might gather, for example, an entrance to a ballpark stadium, a grocery store, or a bus station. The volunteer marks off the boundaries of the space by walking around it in complete silence and then mimes an action that tells the others what that space represents. For instance, the student might start miming the selling of hot dogs at a ballpark. As soon as the members of the class understand the context, they put up their hand to be chosen to enter the space to augment the scene. For example, one person can buy a hot dog. Another might go out onto the field and pretend to be the short stop in a baseball game. There is no talking, only mimed action.

When five or six people are interacting in the scene, touch a student lightly on the shoulder and indicate to him or her that he or she is to change the situation by miming something completely different. For instance, the student could change the ballpark scene to a scene in a hospital emergency room. The seven students who are at the ball game need to become aware of the change of scene and react accordingly. They might cluster around a patient, as they take on the roles of doctors, nurses, technicians, and so on. As this scene establishes itself, the teacher chooses another student to go in and change the scene again. The teacher can ask everyone to leave the scene and the game can start over. After the game has been played several times, invite the students to respond to a variety of follow-up questions, such as:

- When did you notice that the scene had changed?
- How difficult was it for you to realize that the scene had changed?
- What did you have to do to be aware of other people in the scene?
- How aware are we of the actions and behaviors of other people in real life?

Hearing the Absent Voices

Tell the students to play the previous game, but this time the volunteer will be given a piece of paper that will change his or her status, role, or ability. The volunteer will enter the space and change the dynamics by needing something in order to be more comfortable. For instance, the person who enters the ballpark might be in a wheelchair and will therefore need special care. If the students have created a party scene, the volunteer might play someone who has had a drug or alcohol overdose and the students will have to recognize this and react to the crisis. If the scene takes place on a city street, the volunteer might play the role of a homeless person who is desperate for water or a subway fare.

Play the game in silence; then play it again *but allow only the volunteer to speak*. Pose follow-up questions to students, for example:

- When did you notice that the person who had entered the scene was different from you in some way?
- How did hearing the voice of the volunteer make you feel?
- How did you respond when you heard the voice of someone who is usually silenced in our society?

- Did you think that she/he was looked after adequately by the other role-players in the scene?
- What might they have done differently?
- How do we tend to react to people who disrupt our lives or disturb what we are doing?
- What are our ethical responsibilities toward such people?
- Do any of you have a story that seems connected to this exercise that you would like to share?

Let Me Introduce You To…

Students stand in a circle facing in. Ask them to think of someone who they believe has changed the world for the better because of that individual's actions and beliefs. They need to know some facts about this person (for example, Martin Luther King Jr., Nelly McClung, Mahatma Ghandi, Anne Frank). They imagine that this person is beside them. They mingle with others in the circle and introduce themselves and their chosen hero/heroine to a classmate. As soon as they have made the introductions, they exchange names of heroes/heroines with a partner and then find someone else to introduce that person to. Model the exercise first, for example:

> Hello, my name is Kathy and I want to introduce you to Rosa Parks. Rosa Parks was a courageous black woman who, in 1955, refused to give up her seat on a bus to a white passenger. She was arrested by the police and the outrage in response to Rosa's unfair treatment contributed significantly to the American Civil Rights Movement.
>
> OR
>
> Hi, I'd like you to meet Chief Dan George, who was a gifted actor and chief of the Tsleil-waututh Nation in Burrard Inlet, British Columbia….

The students continue to exchange information and the names of their heros/heroines for as long as is feasible. They then re-group in the circle and introduce the last person to whom they were introduced. After the game, you can ask students to tell you the names of some of the people to write on the board and then categorize the individuals, create research groups, share biographies in class, and so on.

I am From…/We are From…

Probably one of the most successful writing exercises that I use with groups of students is called "I am from…/We are from…." By means of various prompts, the students are given an opportunity to examine the kinds of places, signposts, symbols, people, relationships, choices, words, images, food, celebrations, beliefs, sayings, and experiences that have shaped who they are at the moment and who and what they are becoming. The prompts can be changed depending on the audience. A number of extensions can be adapted to many different teaching scenarios and subjects.

I hand out a lined index card to each student. I have them sit by themselves and I tell them that the exercise they are about to do will allow them to respond spontaneously to some prompts to help them reflect on the kinds of experiences and encounters that have shaped their identities. I tell them that they are going to work independently at first and then with a partner. I encourage them to let their memories and imaginations run at full speed and I tell them not to worry about what they are going to write. The writing can always be revised. They can also experiment with new ideas and forms of writing, if they wish.

I ask students to write "I am from..." at the top of the index cards. Then, modeling the kinds of things that I would write about myself, I ask them to record answers to the prompts that I give to them, for example:

- Write down your favorite thing to eat. Describe some of its characteristics if you can. (*I am from macaroni and cheese with breadcrumbs on top, fresh out of the oven.*)
- Think about your journey to school every day. Record the stores, parks, or landmarks you pass on the way to school. (*I am from the coffee shop on the corner of Elm and Princess Streets.*)
- Write down a favorite family saying. (Sayings can be written in the student's first language.)
- Describe an old toy or a keepsake that you will never throw away (for example, a model car, a photograph, a concert ticket stub).
- Describe the place where you keep that special item. (*in a drawer in my bedside table; in my wallet; on a shelf in the garage*)
- Name the place you wish you could return to when you have more time and/or money. (*My grandmother's home in Jamaica.*)
- Think about holiday food, songs, and traditions. Describe them. (*I am from tourtière on New Year's Eve.*)
- Write about daily happenings. (*I am from an alarm clock that always rings right on the dot of 6 a.m.*)

Next, students find a partner and share their "I am from ..." responses. I usually give students 10 to 15 minutes to share what each of their responses means. You will find that they have lots to tell one another!

Then, I invite them to combine their responses so that their voices and the words, images, and meanings work together to make a "We are from ..." poem. I encourage them to change words, delete lines, add more poetic language, or repeat images. They are also invited to add lines and words that provide more information in artistic ways. Then I ask them to find ways to read their lines. They might decide to read the poem chorally and to layer sounds or sound effects. I ask them to pay attention to the silences in the poem as well, and to learn how to pause for effect. Eventually, they find a way to move their bodies to reflect the words that they have created.

Finally, I ask students to share the favorite lines that they have created together. Some share entire poems.

I have done this exercise in many different ways with many different groups: adult English Language Learners; the students from the "Imagine a School..." project; junior grade students; teacher candidates; and all kinds of teachers from all kinds of schools and school districts. I encourage everyone to think of their own unique prompts.

Here are the prompts that I used with some Ontario Arts Council artists who were enrolled in a non-degree certificate course in Arts Education for Artists working in Ontario schools:

I am from…
a **decision** that was made for me or a decision that I made myself that changed the course of my life.

I am from…
the **place** where I create my art.

I am from…
the **tools** that I use to create my art.

I am from...
a **time** that I think back to regularly with happiness and hope.

I am from…
a person or people who was/were there for me when I needed help.

I am from…
an incident that happened in my life that made me rethink who I am and what I need to become.

I am from…
the kindest gesture anyone ever showed me.

I am from…
A relationship that has shaped me into the person that I am now.

I am from…
words that matter.

When I worked with actors from the Stratford Festival of Canada who were involved in a similar course, I added the following prompts:

I am from…
favorite lines in a play that I remember with ease and pleasure.

I am from…
the **stage** that I stood on when I said those lines.

While working with the students in the "Imagine a School…" project, I asked them to write about where they were from in terms of their own school experiences:

I am from…
the words that I hear in the hallways of my school;
the nicest thing a teacher ever said to me;
what my parents expect me to accomplish in the future;
the words of my high school motto.

Another approach is to use numbers as prompts, for example:

I am from…
the numbers two and four:
two mothers; two fathers; two sisters; two cousins; two cats;
two times two makes four.

I am from…
four grandmothers; four grandfathers; four stepbrothers and sisters;
I was born on the fourth of March.
I have four close friends: Mandeep, Annie, Claire, and Chui.
Four divided by two is two.

I have two identities:
Cree and Newfoundlander.

I am from…
One mother
Two fathers
Three grandparents
Four brothers
Five rooms in my apartment
Six doors
Seven teachers who support me
Eight close friends
Nine cousins
Ten people on my soccer team.

As another variation on this exercise, one of my colleagues, Marni Binder, invites her students to create quilts in which the design is based on a personal artifact or memento. She often asks students to create an "I am from…" poem to accompany their quilts.

I once worked with a Grade 10 class who were reading *A Raisin in the Sun* in their English program. I developed the following prompts to have them revisit the play to investigate some of the imagery, setting, language, and relationships in detail:

> Pick a character—either Walter or Ruth—whom you have met in the first scene of the play. Write "I am from…" at the top of the card.
>
> I am from… [physical characteristics].
> I am from… [the most important object in the apartment to me].
> I am from… [the line that I said that defines my character].
> I am from… [the line that was said to me that hurt me the most].

Sample Student Responses

> I am from… *disappointment that has already begun to hang in my face.*
> I am from… *the pot of water that I boil every morning.*
> I am from… *Eat your eggs, they gonna be cold.*
> I am from… *just for a second you looked real young again.*
> I am **Ruth**.
>
> I am from… *mismatched pajamas that define my life.*
> I am from… *the newspaper that brings us nothing but bad news.*
> I am from… *This morning I was lookin' in the mirror and thinking about it.… I am thirty-five years old; I been married eleven years and I got a boy who sleeps in the living room—and all I got to give him is stories about how rich white people live.*

I am from… *Honey, you never say nothing new.*
I am **Walter**.

I encouraged the students to find a way to combine each of the lines into a poem. Below is one brilliant example.

We are from… *mismatched pajamas that hang with disappointment.*
We are from… *pots of water boiling over with bad news.*
We are from… *This morning I was lookin' in the mirror and thinking about it… Eat your eggs, they gonna be cold; I am thirty-five years old; Eat your eggs; I been married eleven years and I got a boy who sleeps in the living room; they gonna be cold; and all I got to give him is stories about how rich white people live; Eat your eggs, they gonna be cold.*
We are from… *Just for a second you looked real young again. Honey, you never say nothing new.*
We are **Walter** and **Ruth** in *A Raisin in the Sun.*

By Jerome and Kiara

The students found a way to read their poems and we shared all sorts of impressions of the very first scene in the play.

Lay Your Cards on the Table: Images of Identity

Students learn though active engagement. They need to create and co-create knowledge for themselves. They need to feel comfortable sharing their experiences and identities with one another. Belarie Zatzman, Associate Dean in the Faculty of Fine Arts at York University, has taught me that identity is not fixed. On the contrary, identity is shaped, reaffirmed, and nurtured by relational interactions with everything and everyone that we meet along our life's journey: people, places, communities, relationships, culture, beliefs, language, artwork, texts, and so on. Identity is fluid and culturally assertive. As such, there can never be only one interpretation of who we are because our identities change in response to the different situations and contexts in which we find ourselves.

The "Lay Your Cards on the Table" exercise invites students to reflect on different aspects of their identities and to share information about themselves and the world in which they live. Ample time is needed for this activity because the conversations that ensue require active listening and sensitive responses. Much of this activity has to do with bearing witness to who we are as a community of human beings who live and interact in a complex world. The exercise allows participants to find out what they have in common with each other, how they differ from each other, how exclusion has affected them, and how a sense of belonging and acceptance are motivators for learning.

This exercise allows students to tell us something important about themselves and their experiences. I have adapted this exercise from ones conducted regularly in equity workshops sponsored by the Toronto District School Board along with one I learned from a colleague, Alice Te, an Equity Instructional Leader and teacher in the Toronto District School Board. I do this exercise with students in classrooms and teachers in workshops because it allows all participants to understand their "location" in terms of their own identities and to recognize how this understanding shapes their view of themselves and how it conditions them to interpret the world. It serves to introduce participants to other ways of thinking, believing, and interacting. (*Note*: This exercise usually takes a fair amount of time so I do not use it with students or teachers unless I know that I have a good chunk of time—at least an hour or more—to work with them.)

1. First, as a group, we brainstorm what we mean by "identity" and we write our ideas on the board or on chart paper. We usually decide on a definition of "identity" that looks something like this:

   Identity = the set of behavioral or personal characteristics by which an individual is recognizable as a member of a group

   We talk about how identities can change—how fluid and adaptable they are. I remind students that they can identify themselves by their gender, age, ethnicity, race, religion, sexual orientation, position in their family constellation (for example, middle child); the team they are on, what they do in their spare time; what they value; their religious or spiritual beliefs; and so on.

2. I hand out six unlined index cards to each person. Then I ask participants to write their name on the first card in large letters. On each of the next five cards, I ask them to write down the aspects of their identity *that are most important to them.* They do this silently and independently. As facilitator, I make sure that I am available to help them if necessary. If they would like more cards to round out who they are, I hand them out.

   When students have finished recording aspects of their identities, I ask them to flip each card over and draw an image that connects to this aspect of their identity in some way. If they have identified themselves as a member of a hockey team, for example, they might draw a hockey net or a hockey stick. If they are an urban dweller, they might sketch a cityscape; if they are Jewish, they might sketch a menorah. I tell the participants not to worry about the quality of their artwork but to sketch something quickly that has a meaning connected to the group to which they have identified.

   I ask the students to lay their cards before them on their desks with the artwork either face down and the identity word face up, or vice versa. Then they begin playing with the formation and structure of the cards. For instance, they can put their name in the middle of the card collage or at the top of a pile of cards. They can prioritize their identities or overlap them. They can flip cards over and juxtapose sketches. Their desk becomes a *gallery of identity* that has to make sense to them.

3. I then ask the participants to get into groups of five. They collect their cards into a pack (I call it their "identity pack") and take them with them into the group. They lay their name cards down on a group table; they then take turns sharing their cards with the group. I advise students to choose only the cards that they feel comfortable talking about. They can set aside the cards that are private and personal if they wish. They are allowed to pass and just listen, but I encourage them to become involved in the exercise. As they lay their cards out on the table and talk about their identities, experiences, and feelings, the conversations are never rushed.

4. Next, I ask students to think of a time when being a member of one of these particular groups made them feel included and valued. They choose one card and write words that are connected to that memory around the margins of the card. For the second card, they choose a category that made

them feel excluded. They write words that describe how it felt to be excluded. They then share their stories of inclusion and exclusion, if they wish, in the small groups.

5. We then use the cards to make a word wall showing all the categories and the words describing the feelings associated with Inclusion/Exclusion. The word wall could look something like this:

Identity	How did it feel when you were excluded?	How did it feel when you were included?
Academic Success	Angry	Proud
Socio-Economic Status	Resentful	Secure
Age	Hurt	Special
Learning Disability	Frustrated	Comfortable
Sexual Orientation	Lonely	Recognized
Clothing	Different	Different
Physical Appearance	Confused	Confident
Neighborhood	Isolated	Happy
Moral Values	Inferior	Excited
Gender Identity	Worthless	Trusted
Body Size	Invisible	Cared For
Race	Substandard	Liked
Political Beliefs	Unwanted	Accepted
Accent	Untrustworthy	Appreciated
Learning Styles	Unaccepted	Reinforced
Gender	Closed	Trustworthy
Colour	Ashamed	Loved
Physical Dis/ability	Rejected	Grateful
Technological Knowledge		Belonging
Popularity		Open
Ethnicity		Positive
Athletic Ability		Nurtured
Geographic Origin		Important
Introvert/Extrovert		Responsible
Language		Grown-up
Family Demographics		Respected
Religion		
Music Preferences		
Food Restrictions		
Immigration Status		

6. The final reflection piece can take many forms. You can work with the whole class first and then ask the students to write independent reflections, or you can combine both approaches. Here are some suggestions:

Questions for the Whole Class
- What common identity factors did you notice in your group?
- What are some ways in which we differ from each other in this class? In what ways are we similar?
- Why is it important to acknowledge these similarities and differences amongst us?

- What impact will this knowledge have on our cooperative work together as a class?
- When we do exercises like this, what do we learn about ourselves and others? What do we learn about living in the world?
- How might you feel/act differently because of the new knowledge that you acquired through this exercise?
- What kinds of communication and interaction in the group might change because of what we just shared together? Why do you think that might happen?

Independent Reflection

- Was this an easy or a difficult exercise for you to do? What factors made it easy or difficult?
- Were you surprised by the identities that you chose for yourself?
- Did you learn something about another person's identity that you did not know about before?
- Would other people such as your friends and families have written down other identities for you? Why is it that others see us differently from how we see ourselves?

"Protecting Our Students Into Understanding"

Internationally renowned drama educator Dorothy Heathcote has taught me to "protect my students into understanding." This means that although I set the standards high for myself and for my students, I get to know my students as individuals as I teach them and I usually discover that they need different kinds of support to get to the place where they need to be. I recognize that some of my students are fragile; thus, I need to work slowly and deliberately—I protect them as they reveal themselves to me.

Students learn best in conditions that offset fear and isolation and that foster trust, a sense of adventure, and healthy risk-taking. In the inclusive and respectful classroom community that my students and I build together, I demonstrate control but not regimentation. I know that the first and most important strategy is to get to know my students and to try to understand them from the inside out.

4

Critical Thinking and Emotional Literacy (Elementary)

What Do We Do With a Variation?

What do we do with a difference?
Do we stand and discuss its oddity
or do we ignore it?

Do we shut our eyes to it
or poke it with a stick?
Do we clobber it to death?

Do we move around it in rage
and enlist the rage of others?
Do we will it to go away?

Do we look at it in awe
or purely in wonderment?
Do we work for it to disappear?

Do we pass it stealthily
or change route away from it?
Do we will it to become like ourselves?

What do we do with a difference?
Do we communicate to it,
let application acknowledge it
for barriers to fall down?

James Berry

What *do* we do with a difference? This is one of the central questions in social justice education, because it acknowledges that in most societies, one set of cultural norms, traditions, and values tends to dominate over another. Teachers need to help students develop a critical awareness of the privilege that one culture often possesses over another and to investigate what that means for people who cannot benefit from the advantage. In *Drama and Diversity* (2000), Sharon Grady writes: "While a grand idea, democracy is fraught with the humanistic desire for wholeness and equality that can never quite be attained because unequal power dynamics are impossible to escape. Perhaps the best we can do is be willing and able to recognize power, acknowledge bias, work towards understanding, and know that it is a constant and daily struggle."

I am interested in working with students from the inside out. I want them to understand human relationships, power dynamics, multiple perspectives, complex ideas, and intense feelings by imagining themselves in other people's shoes for a while—thinking, feeling, speaking, writing, drawing, and moving as if they were another person in another time and place. I then encourage them to step away from the imagined experience, reflecting on it and ultimately attaining an understanding of something different about the world and about other people's lives.

I use drama-in-education strategies as I work from within stories of people who have been treated unjustly. I challenge my students to find the silent voices in both texts and images and to bring those voices to the forefront. By doing so, we can hear people who have been silenced tell us what we need to know as we strive to create a fair and just society. I ask students to step into the stories through drama to unlock power dynamics and to ignite conversations about human differences. We spend time questioning the word "tolerance" and the uneven power dynamic that the word implies. The work is intense and sometimes difficult as students confront their own biases in the time for reflection that I weave throughout the lessons.

Why do I work this way? I believe that the capacity to experience something from another person's perspective is directly linked to critical thinking and emotional literacy. We all have the human capacity to move between imagination and reality, and drama provides a safe haven for students to explore issues related to social justice. The metaphor of walking in someone else's shoes in order to understand another person's experience is a strategy that allows us to imagine that person's reality. When we discover from the inside out that other people often do not have the same access to the future that we do, we understand the need to advocate for social justice on their behalf.

Drama, Empathy, and Point of View

Drama is a medium that facilitates richly structured learning about how humans live in the world. Through role-playing, students benefit from the sense of freedom and security that allows them to pretend to be someone else for a while and to feel exempt from life's immediate pressures. By involvement in drama, students work together to build an imagined context in which real feelings and ideas are explored safely because the students are acting "in role." Students discover that they can plan, shape, control, and reflect upon their experiences by "living through" another person's dilemma and by talking and writing about it afterwards. The students' deep immersion in drama derives from their ability to step inside someone else's reality for a while, to empathize with that person, and then to spend time reflecting on that imagined experience. Both during and after the drama, students offer insights into how the story, the relationships, or the situation could have had a different outcome if the characters had behaved differently.

By means of drama, I encourage my students to see the world in a different light. They gain new information and examine it critically; they see facts illuminated in various and sometimes contradictory ways. I want my students to learn how to become conscious of another person's reality—to see and feel from

Drama allows students to "listen to the silenced, talk with the powerless, see beneath the stereotype and hear beyond the rhetoric."

Brian Edminston

inside someone else's situation or relationship. Drama shows them that they have an ability to see the world through an array of different lenses.

In drama, we can adjust the lenses. For example, we can focus on the most powerful lines in a poem, on a character's final words in a script, on the interplay between images and text in a graphic novel, or on the most perplexing visual in a picture book. We can then use our bodies and our voices to bring the images and written words alive. We can turn back time and create scenes that might have happened before the story began, or we can fast-forward into a scene in the future in order to "live through," as it were, the consequences of a character's actions. We can create new characters who did not appear in the original story and interview them to hear their silent voices, thereby gaining an entirely fresh perspective. We can interpret events, issues, feelings, and ideas through movement; we can watch for hesitancy in a character's speech and wonder what is causing that uncertainty. We can ask "What happens if…?" and "What happens when…?" so that students can use their imaginations to see an incident, a person, a theme, an idea, or a relationship more astutely. David Booth, Professor Emeritus at the Ontario Institute for Studies in Education, has helped me to understand drama's potential to set up "complex and different contexts that allow us to enter the 'as if, what if' world and thus become transformed by who we meet, what we witness, where we journey, and what we experience" (Booth, 2003).

Finding Our Voices Through Drama

Language is the tool that we employ in an attempt to control our lives and to initiate action. In drama, language is at the core of human experience. When students assume roles, they expand their language power. The contexts offered by drama encourage students to explore social functions of language that they might otherwise not encounter in a traditional classroom. Drama allows students to find language that portrays their most passionate ideas and values. It also gives them an opportunity to use vocabulary, speech registers, and language structures that are new to them.

Students gain confidence as they talk about the experiences and ideas that have been generated both within and outside the drama. The overall social well-being of the class is enhanced as students work together to solve problems, think deeply about another person's point of view, investigate new ideas, explore parallel universes, role-play characters, and discuss their reactions to the drama from their own points of view.

Exploring Silent Voices Through Drama

> I want American history taught. Unless I'm in that book, you're not in it either. History is not a procession of illustrious people. It's about what happens to a people. Millions of anonymous people is what history is about.
>
> James Baldwin

The work done in drama is intense and the reflection afterwards is crucial in moving students to a fuller understanding of life's intricacies, difficulties, and ambiguities. Through drama, I help my students become aware of the many silent voices in the world. As we employ drama techniques to explore works of literature, I ask them to reflect on questions such as:

- Whose voices are present?
- Whose voices are absent?
- What can we learn about the human condition by becoming involved in these stories?
- To whom in the story do we relate, and why?
- What connections can we make between the story and our own personal narratives?

As teachers, it is our job to "unshackle thought" (Maxine Greene) so that students can experience an informed encounter with the themes in the material with which they are working, whether the source material is a script, a poem, an excerpt from a novel, a letter, or a newspaper article. We can prepare them for this encounter with the text so that they emerge from our classrooms more eloquent, more knowledgeable, and more analytical than they were before the lessons. Drama is meant to provoke conversations—and the discussions about issues of race, power, inclusion, and exclusion should happen before, during, and after the drama, in classrooms where students feel safe to talk about difficult concepts in relation to their own lives.

When students come to know and understand people unlike themselves and to think critically and compassionately about other people's realities, they become more informed about how the world works. My experience as a drama teacher has led me into many classrooms in which students end up telling me: "But if you think about it from his perspective…"; "If you spent some time listening to the voices in her head…"; "If you stood in their shoes for a while…"; "I thought I understood this idea/event/relationship/person/time in history but I see it differently now because it was as if I were there." Sometimes students make comments such as: "Ah, yes. That is something that I have experienced." They witness their initial understandings, ideas, and opinions about the world either confirmed or transformed by having lived through an imagined experience in which they are challenged to think, feel, speak, and write in role as someone similar to and yet unlike themselves.

Situations in the drama might remind them of their own hurts and struggles, of their own stories and relationships, and of their own identities and life-changing experiences. Conversely, the drama might present them with previously unknown possibilities. Students sometimes respond: "I never knew that people could act this way. This is beyond my imagining. This is something new for me to witness." They might ask: "Could this really be the way that it was? Is this what slavery was really like? Why do I feel so uncomfortable, so angry, and so frustrated? What can we do about situations like this that occur in real life?"

Part of the mandate of drama is to bear witness. A certain responsibility always accompanies the work that students and teachers do together in the classroom. It is important to bear witness to the injustices that we explore in and through drama, and to share with others what we have observed and experienced. Opportunities for reflection following work in drama are critical in helping students understand how difficult life is for many people and how vital it is to advocate for everyone's place in history, for their voice in the present, and for their imprint on the future.

Sometime in your life, hope that you might see one starved man, the look on his face when the bread finally arrives. Hope that you might have baked it or bought or even kneaded it yourself. For that look on his face, for your meeting his eyes across a piece of bread, you might be willing to lose a lot, or suffer a lot, or die a little, even.

Daniel Berrigan

To bear witness is to speak for others to others.

Paul Cela

Drama and Equity Education

My journey as teacher and board administrator has allowed me to make strong connections between drama methodologies and equity education policies. A focus on making inclusive curriculum a priority for schools was initiated by the Toronto Board of Education in the early 1990s. The Board's Equity Studies Department and the Drama Department co-developed many workshops, seminars, and courses related to anti-racist education. In 1993, the Equity Studies Department helped me plan and teach a three-year Additional Teaching Qualification course at the Faculty of Education of the University of Toronto. The course was titled "Anti-racist Education Through Drama." In the course, I shared my expertise in drama with teachers and administrators who had been working in anti-racist/equity education for several years and who had carved out strong reputations as equity educators.

The teachers enrolled in the Additional Teaching Qualification course had recently been introduced to drama in their schools through an in-service program called "Partners in Drama" coordinated by the Toronto Board of Education's Drama Department. In this program, artists and teachers partnered with each other and taught the curriculum through drama. During the project, participants developed a strong belief in drama as one of the most effective ways to teach students about equity issues. They had seen clear evidence of drama's potential for teaching students about other ways of looking at the world as they explored social justice issues depicted in stories, picture books, novels, historical documents, and newspaper accounts of current events. At the end of the program, the teachers requested a more in-depth study of drama as a methodology for use in anti-discriminatory teaching. Thus evolved the "Anti-racist Education Through Drama" course.

All the teachers in the course were committed to improving the effectiveness of drama in their classrooms and they wished to partner with a colleague in their school to facilitate ongoing dialogue about equity education through drama. They wished to transform their schools into places of professional study so that they could practice the methodologies they were learning in the course, confer with their colleagues about their learning, and bring questions and insights back to the group.

Teaching for equity and social justice through drama linked the various cross-curricular approaches to education that challenge racism, sexism, ethnocentrism, homophobia, classism, ageism, and discrimination against persons with disabilities. By the end of the first year of the course, the teachers and I had identified four big questions that we wanted to explore together:

1. How do we build communities of learning through drama in such a way that all voices are heard and valued?
2. How do we gain awareness of the varied backgrounds and cultures of our students and celebrate that diversity?
3. How do we eliminate discriminatory behavior in schools on the part of both teachers and students?
4. How do we address the systemic imbalances of freedom and access within the educational system?

Windows, Mirrors, and Doors: Using Metaphors in Equity Education

While teaching the course in "Anti-racist Education Through Drama," I introduced my students to the work that academics Emily Styles and Peggy McIntosh were doing related to the SEEDS Project at Wellesley College in Toronto. These educators view curriculum as a kind of architectural structure that schools build around students. Styles' metaphor of curriculum as window and mirror complements McIntosh's ideas about multiple perspectives in education. Their combined thinking promotes a view of curriculum that provides students with opportunities to see not only the realities of others (curriculum as "window") but also representations of their own realities (curriculum as "mirror"). When curriculum is conceptualized in this way, human differences as well as commonalities are validated, and students' understanding of themselves in relation to others expands.

Styles and McIntosh encourage students and teachers to talk about "the textbooks of their lives" in order to inform conversations in their communities about education and culture. They stress that everyone's story needs to be heard and they recognize that respectful teacher education can help make the teaching of equity in our schools respectful and effective as well.

As the course progressed and as trust grew within our group, I asked the teachers to tell one another their stories and, through their personal journals, describe how the drama activities and exercises were affecting them not only as teachers but also as people.

When Peggy Macintosh introduced the window and mirror metaphors to the Curriculum and Program Division of the Toronto Board of Education in the mid-1990s, I immediately saw a connection between these metaphors and drama. I developed a third metaphor, the door. I began to use this metaphor in the course as well as in my subsequent work in drama-in-education with the Toronto District School Board.

The door is a powerful metaphor because of its nature and function. Doors can be left ajar, they can be opened wide, and they can be shut for private discussion. In drama, we can step through a door into other landscapes and see the world from different perspectives. Screen doors let in light and air and allow us to view people, situations, and issues from a distance, filtering out impurities so that we can see things more clearly. Half-doors permit drama teachers to hide some of the truth in order to illuminate other parts of the story. There are outside doors, storm doors, and doors with glass that split light into prisms to symbolize life's ambiguities and multiple realities. Revolving doors help us come full circle in our understanding of the complexities and nuances of the human condition. Sometimes the doors won't budge and we, as teachers, must try to push them open. We need many strategies up our sleeves to stimulate critical thinking and to transform hearts and minds. Sometimes, the door stays jammed and we must find new ways to open it. Sometimes a door is locked and we must figure out how to find a key to open it safely so we can see what's on the other side.

Throughout the course, I began to look for doors in the source material and strategies that I was using with the teachers. The door became a powerful framing device and it helped me locate stories with dramatic potential. I discovered strategies for structuring a story's framework, changing how the light shone on topics under discussion, and screening out what was not relevant in my lessons. I found ways to close doors from time to time so my students could talk about characters and issues in private.

Drama strategies that permitted safe exploration, creation, and representation of ideas became the mainstay of the course. Doors can act as symbols for people who have been treated unjustly. They often provide ways for people to describe the exclusion they have experienced. Using the door metaphor to feel safe as we explored difficult issues pertaining to racism and prejudice became very important. When our students were safely in role, we could examine the injustice depicted in the stories and other source material we were studying with some measure of detachment. The drama teacher's role as the doorkeeper was essential. In adopting this role, we began to make some important decisions about the use of drama to teach anti-racist material. We questioned casting students in the role of the racist or the perpetrator of racism. We felt more comfortable putting students in enabling roles, such as the opponent of racism, the protector of the victim, or the onlooker who has to make decisions about how to behave when confronting racism.

The Treasure Chest Project

What became clear as the "Anti-Racist Education Through Drama" course wound up was that we needed a resource document to bring together all the ideas we had been exploring. Thus began the writing of *The Treasure Chest* document. Teachers, artists, and leaders in education began to write and field test the material that we had been using both within and outside the course. As we gathered more books and ideas, we began to record our work in writing. We used the stories we had selected as a basis of dramatic exploration (Booth, 1994). Many of our lessons were developed in the Drama/Dance Project, a program in which students participated in drama and dance for an eight-day period with a drama facilitator and dancers at the Canadian Children's Dance Theatre. The material that we developed reflected solid equity policy embedded within imaginative drama and dance lessons that could help teachers teach drama and dance while at the same time exploring issues of bullying, inequity, and systemic injustice.

The Woman Who Outshone the Sun

One of the lessons in *The Treasure Chest* presents an archetypal stranger, Lucia Zenteno, the heroine of the bilingual book *The Woman Who Outshone the Sun/La Mujer que brillaba aun mas que el sol* by Alejandro Cruz Martinez. Lucia lives in a community from which she is excluded because of her strangeness and her magical powers. All doors are closed to her. The villagers spy on her day and night and keep their distance from her. They live behind doors of ignorance and mistrust. Eventually, the villagers drive Lucia out of the village. When she leaves, however, the river that sustains the village flows into Lucia's hair and travels with her. The village is left with "only a dry winding riverbed, a serpent of sand where the water had been." This story allows teachers to employ all three metaphors in teaching about equity: the window, the mirror, and the door.

What are the windows in this story? What are Lucia's origins? What kind of society has she tried to enter? Why does her unique beauty and mysterious strength anger and frighten the people with whom she comes in contact? What magical powers does she possess? Why and how does she remain so unbowed and dignified? Who are some real people whose lives remind us of Lucia's? As we examine the story of Lucia Zenteno, we can discover many things. We can retell her story from the perspective of objects that were left behind in her home in order to achieve a new frame of reference. In one Grade 8 class I taught, a girl held the collar of Lucia's dress and told the story from the point of view of the collar, remembering the "unbearable burden of being close to Lucia" when the protagonist felt excluded and rejected. This student gave voice to her feelings of sadness and fear at Lucia's plight, but she also celebrated Lucia's strength and integrity.

What are the mirrors in this story? When the story is read out loud in Spanish, how do those who speak Spanish as a first language respond? What is the reaction of those listeners who hear the words but do not as yet understand their meaning? What is the response of the Spanish-speaking Guatemalan student who has just arrived in Canada and is invited to read the story out loud to the class? How does she feel when the class spontaneously erupts in applause to express their appreciation of the fluency and power of her oral presentation? What are the teacher's reactions to the comments written by students after working in drama with this story? One Grade 8 student composed the following journal entry in response to the story:

> I learned that…
>
> you can be beautiful and have black hair
>
> you can have enormous power and be a woman
>
> you can be fat and still be considered dangerous because of your beauty
>
> you can carry on with your life and make choices even when you are being discriminated against

What doors open up a deeper understanding of this story? If we peer through a metaphorical screen door, can we perceive Lucia's essence? What can we do to prompt students to wonder why Lucia would be treated so badly? How can this story help change readers' attitudes and behavior toward people who suffer persecution and rejection because they are different?

If we explore the story from the inside out and if we return to the place of Lucia's origin and adopt the role of her protectors, what will we discover? What will we learn about her suffering? What will we remember about her past triumphs? What insight into her powers might we gain? What will we begin to understand about our shared humanity?

And when one of the village elders who had exiled Lucia follows her to her place of origin and demands to have the water back, what will we, as Lucia's protectors, say to the elder? How can we teach students that not only Lucia and her tormentors suffer but that everyone in a community suffers when someone is ostracized? Lucia withdraws into exile and seclusion. Lucia's protectors suffer as they witness a member of their community treated cruelly. The villagers suffer from the emotional and spiritual poverty inherent in their detachment from Lucia.

Inclusion/Exclusion

In one secondary school classroom in which students living with a mental illness were integrated into the program, I worked with the story of Lucia Zenteno over several days. I invited the students to retell the story in small groups. I asked them to create tableaux to represent the event that forced Lucia from the village. We explored Lucia's extraordinary journey home through movement and music. On the third day, the students, in their roles as Lucia's protectors, decided to speak to Lucia about returning to the village. However, one girl made us stop before we invited Lucia to speak. She declared: "But we must remember that the powers that allowed Lucia to take the water are not under her control. No one can force Lucia to give the water back. The villagers who were so cruel to her must learn compassion. They must be patient and learn from her." The protectors were reluctant to have Lucia return to the village alone. One boy suggested that some of the protectors accompany her as the "Scouts in the Forest." They would monitor the behavior of the villagers to make sure that the community treated Lucia with respect.

In the discussion that followed the role-play, the students living with a mental illness discussed how they have been treated as people on the margins of society. Although they had been silenced and stigmatized, they realized that often their understanding of human behavior is deeply insightful. They recognized that the perpetrators of the bullying or the discrimination that they encounter in their own lives are like the villagers—people who have the power to drive others out because the system allows them to do so. Unless we can help people recognize the loss that all communities experience as a result of exclusion and prejudice, those who hold power will remain insensitive to other points of view. The victims will remain silent. All of us lose out when society is allowed to marginalize some of its members.

The dry winding riverbed—symbolizing a loss of vitality—is what our schools, our communities, and our society will become unless we learn to value difference, welcome it, nurture it, and celebrate the beauty, wealth, and strength in it. Styles and McIntosh remind us how limiting it is to educate our students provincially when they must live their lives in a global context. We must therefore find ways to help all students recognize and celebrate differences and similarities in the people and cultures with whom they will have contact, as they mature and become socially responsible adults. Teachers can use the framing devices of both windows and mirrors to teach students ways of knowing about and reflecting back the world and the people who enrich it. Finally, teachers can employ the metaphor of the door in drama to safely illuminate issues of culture, language, inclusion, and exclusion as part of the process of teaching all students about one another and the diverse world in which we live. By using these metaphors in our teaching, we can accomplish what activist and humanitarian Terry Waite (1994) urges us all to do: *to work for the weak to be strong, the strong to be just, and the just to be compassionate.*

Architecture of the Imagination

I'll describe another example of the power of drama to allow silent voices to be heard. I once worked with some Grade 8 students on a relatively long-term, integrated arts project called Architecture of the Imagination. The work was linked to Saskia Olde Wolbers' exhibition at the Art Gallery at York University. (Wolbers is a Dutch contemporary video artist who now lives in London, England.) The students spent two mornings at the gallery viewing her films. Then they participated in art activities, drama, storytelling, and video production

We say, "A person is a person through other persons." I need you in order to be me and you need me in order to be you.

Desmond Tutu

sessions at York University, at Brookview Middle School, and at Charles Street Video, one of Toronto's leading artist-run video production centers.

During the first phase of the project, dub poet Michael St. George and I helped students develop narratives to form the basis of voiceover scripts for the videos they would ultimately produce. Michael was determined that the stories that the students created should derive from their own experiences. He told his own story of growing up in Jamaica and he helped students see how they could make their experiences come alive through the magic of words chosen carefully and artistically. The process was challenging and there were many false starts. Eventually, however, the students found a way of telling us who they are.

These students live in the Jane and Finch area of Toronto, a community comprised primarily of new immigrants to Canada. As members of this community, they struggle with how they have been stereotyped in the media as poor, underprivileged, and violent. They yearn to succeed despite the obstacles that lie in their paths. These students told stories of their families, of their experiences at school, and of their dreams of going to university. In telling their stories, some groups of students chose the route of fantasy—taking us to the moon in a spacecraft or fighting pirates on the high seas. Others told stories that were an amalgam of personal events and narratives they had heard told about people who lived in their community. The students demonstrated incredible dedication to their goals and I observed them became more and more focused as the project became increasingly layered.

During the storywriting stage, students worked with me to strengthen their dramatic performances, rehearsing the script that they would later record as a voiceover off-camera narration for their video productions. Under visual artist Bruno Billio's supervision, students designed miniature sets to serve as a backdrop for their narrative. Using everyday objects, the students experimented with familiar materials, fashioning them to unexpected and imaginative ends. Students were taught how a set can evoke a mood and an atmosphere to enhance a story. The students created storyboards as a way of visually mapping out narrative sequences with corresponding sculpture, drawings, and set designs.

The miniature sets that the students created served as the visual focus for the video production phase, led by video artist Sarah Sharkey Pearce. Students learned video production skills through hands-on exercises that included a pre-production process and a post-production phase. Using a high-definition video camera, students alternated between directing and shooting scenes, experimenting with a variety of camera angles and movements as well as lighting to achieve the desired visual and emotional effects. During the video production stage, students learned how a carefully crafted mise-en-scene can enhance mood and atmosphere and add layers of narrative depth and complexity to a story. Working alongside video editor Aleesa Cohene at Charles Street Video, students participated in the post-production editing process. They decided what footage would be retained and how to combine their video images with their voiceover recording as well as with music.

Once the editing phase was complete, students participated in a voiceover recording session, incorporating the stories they had written into the audio accompaniment for their final video.

Writing in Role as an Object

Because the students were going to tell their story on camera through the use of miniature sets, I had to teach them about symbolism and subtext. In one of the workshops, just after the students had written their stories, I asked them to focus on one object in one of the scenes in their collaborative story. They closed their eyes and allowed their imaginations to roam about the set that they had yet to construct. I asked them to find an object that was the most interesting piece in the set and to examine it from many angles—to step around it in their imaginations and focus on the essential qualities that the object possessed. I allowed them ample time to do this. Then I asked them to open their eyes. I handed out sheets of paper and they divided the sheet into four sections. I asked them to write in role as that object, beginning their writing with the words, "I am…." In the second section of the sheet, they wrote what people saw when they viewed the object. In the third section, they wrote what the object represented to them. In the fourth section, they wrote about what the object symbolized.

Raymond wrote:

> I am a slowly moving rocking chair. When people look at me, they see two paths with no choice. What I really represent is something that does not know which path to pick. Therefore I am symbolic of indecision.

Kevin wrote:

> I am a wallet.
> When people see me, they feel all sorts of emotions.
> What I really represent is something that people love and hate at the same time.
> I am symbolic of status.

Sakishan wrote:

> I am the sun.
> When people see me they see a ball of fire.
> What I really am is the source of all life.
> My symbolism is existence.

Collaborative Art Installation

For the next workshop, I asked students to bring or make an object that would encapsulate the meaning and the message of the story that they were writing. Allyson Adley—the project coordinator from the Art Gallery of York University —had brought some wonderful found objects, including colorful beads, feathers, and stones to augment the class collection. The students placed their objects in the centre of the dance studio at York and pondered how the objects made meaning simply on the basis of juxtaposition to one another. I requested silence and asked students to volunteer to come up and alter the landscape of the objects in any way they wished. As the students observed their classmates changing the positions of the objects, they came to understand how meaning could be manipulated through the rearrangement of symbolic objects.

Talking Ourselves into Understanding

We conducted the last leg of the workshop in the Joan and Martin Goldfarb Centre for Fine Arts. This is a magnificent gallery at York University housing a collection of famous paintings by a number of Canadian and international artists. The gallery evokes a feeling of calm amidst great beauty. I asked for volunteers to stand beside a painting that they liked and to hold the object that they had brought to enhance their storywriting. Devin volunteered first. He had brought a Rubik's cube to the workshop. When I asked him to tell me what the cube symbolized, he held the cube in his hand as he stood beside a painting and said:

> It represents the stereotypes that are used to describe the neighborhood of Jane and Finch. The different sides and the different colors represent the diversity of our neighborhood. People look at us from various angles and see different things. Unless you live in the neighborhood, you don't know what the inside is all about. Things change all the time and you have to live there to understand the patterns of living in the community.

Sofia held a jewelry box and stood beside her painting. She articulated beautifully and poignantly the meaning associated with her object and with the collective story her group had created:

> The day my father left was the day that the party lights went out on the top of the jewelry box. The fun was over. The extras would not happen any more. The party scene balloons popped and the disappointments of life were all around.

All this work culminated with a screening of the students' final videos at York University's new state-of-the-art Price Family cinema. Family and community members, faculty, artists, and students all attended the screening. The audience was amazed by the sophisticated quality of the videos. Here is how two students introduced the productions to the audience; their words speak volumes about the liberating power of art, drama, and storytelling:

> **Tianna and Quan:** Good evening, everyone. My name is Tianna ... and I am Quan.
> **Quan:** We would like to take this opportunity to talk about our experiences throughout this project.
> **Tianna:** We had a really rocky start. This whole thing was new to us; we had no idea that there were videos like the ones that Saskia Olde Wolbers created and we didn't realize how many drafts it would take to write out our stories.
> **Quan:** But in the end, everything worked out and it is what you will see in a few minutes....
> **Tianna:** I think all of us in the class really enjoyed making the sets.
> **Quan:** I loved the smell of the glue gun and paint.
> **Tianna:** She even painted her shoes!
> **Quan:** I really enjoyed getting my hands dirty and being allowed to manipulate color and objects to create redefined items. The objects that we created, such as rocking chairs and paper stars, started out as nothing and then magically became something that held deep meaning.

Tianna: I loved how this opportunity came our way. If this project had not happened, we would not have learned about art, video, storytelling, and drama.

Quan: Without Ms. Williams, this project wouldn't have been possible. So, much thanks to her for letting us borrow her classroom, and, of course, her precious teaching time.

Tianna: Thank you to Michael, Bruno, Aleesa, Sarah, Kathy, and last but not least, Allyson.

Quan and Tianna: Now, our videos are about to be shown, so sit back, relax, and enjoy.

Planning and Teaching With Students in Mind

Garfield Gini-Newman, a professor at the Ontario Institute for Studies in Education at the University of Toronto, reminds us that the material we present to students and the method of presentation can be either "brain compatible" or "brain antagonistic" (Gini-Newman, 2007). Both the content and the pedagogy matter—and to meet the needs of a diverse group of students who have different learning styles, the broader the repertoire of strategies and material that we can draw upon, the more successful we will be. I am always on the lookout for source material that is interesting, thought-provoking, and challenging. I also look for a variety of genres: picture books, newspaper articles, scripts, pamphlets, poetry, visual images, and young adolescent fiction, including graphic novels.

I also try to vary my teaching strategies and to scaffold them carefully as a lesson proceeds. When I plan my lessons, I try to stimulate my students to think in new ways. I might invite them to investigate the bias in a letter to the editor, model their problem-solving skills for younger students, or experiment with a wide range of language styles by creating poetry in unique ways. I encourage them to use different language registers to convey how people think in a given time period, to find alternative endings to a movie or theatre script, and to compare and contrast the way people react to new ideas that challenge the status quo. The methods by which I engage my students in this kind of critical thinking depend on their language development, skill level, ability to work in groups, commitment to the task, and readiness and willingness to interact with thought-provoking material. I need to plan my lessons but I also need to adjust the plan as soon as I meet a particular group of students.

I might have my lesson plan right there in my hands but I am always aware that I might have to adjust or throw out my ideas to teach in the way that meets the needs of the students in my classroom. Speaking at a HOPE conference in Denver, Colorado in October, 2007, Andy Hargreaves referred to what he calls "the Julie Andrews curriculum": "These are a few of my favorite things." It is important to have favorite things—materials, approaches, strategies, assessment tasks—but it is equally important to adjust your favorite things when you need to teach in a way that is more compatible with the needs of your students.

The map is not the territory.

Richard Courtney

The Arrival

As often as possible, it is important to find links between the personal narratives of your students and the material you present to them in class. Who are these students who sit in front of you? Where are they from? What are they thinking and feeling? What is a good way to begin to connect with them so that they can settle in comfortably—so that the agitation of the new classroom experience can lessen?

For the past two summers, I have had the privilege of teaching more than 130 middle school teachers from Jiangsu province in China. They travel to Canada for eight weeks to take a York University course called "Oral Language Development through Drama." They are dedicated educators who are at various levels of English language learning.

On the first day of class, they are jet-lagged and homesick. They do not know each other and hence are very shy with one another, and with me. They are also extremely wary of, if not intimidated by, the active nature of drama. They have never done this kind of work before, either as students or as teachers. Active, cooperative, experiential teaching and learning are new to them. What is even more challenging are drama exercises that propel them into imagined situations in which they have a reason to speak English.

I had been searching for source material that could help me introduce drama concepts in a way that would connect to their lives and not put too much pressure on them in terms of English language fluency. I found it when I discovered *The Arrival* by Shaun Tan.

The Arrival is an immigration story told as a series of wordless images. The story seems to have happened long ago. A man leaves his wife and child in an impoverished town, seeking better prospects in an unknown country on the other side of a vast ocean. He eventually finds himself in a bewildering city of foreign customs, peculiar animals, curious floating objects, and indecipherable languages. With nothing more than a suitcase and a handful of currency, the man finds a place to live, food, and employment. He is helped along the way by sympathetic strangers, each carrying their own unspoken history: stories of struggle and survival in a world of incomprehensible violence, upheaval, and hope. I knew I wanted to use this book with the teachers from Jiangsu and I planned a lesson. However, after my first day with the teachers I realized I needed to do some vocabulary development with them in order to make the drama work successful and satisfying.

I greeted the group on the second day of the course and inquired about their health. They were still very tired, they told me, and there were so many new things to see and do. Toronto beckoned them but also made them uneasy. We wrote down all of their feelings on the chalkboard. We added extra vocabulary by brainstorming suggestions from the group. The teachers seemed delighted to learn more English words and they repeated the words as I wrote them down:

> tired: exhausted, sleepy, enervated
> homesick: longing, wistful, sad
> excited: happy, enthusiastic, thrilled
> nervous: agitated, worried, anxious

I quickly made up an exercise. (If I had thought of it before, I would have displayed the following story on an overhead, but instead I wrote it on the board.) The students copied the story into their notebooks. I called this exercise "Four Times Story Nouns."

FOUR TIMES STORY NOUNS
There was once a young **man**
Who wanted to go on a **trip**
To a **country**
That would be exciting.
This young **man**
Had the **idea**
That the **world**
Would be different from where he had once lived.
But he was wrong.
The **place**
Turned out to be different in some ways and the same in others.
The young **man**
Enjoyed his **time** in his new **country**
But he returned to his **home**
To live out the rest of his **life**
With his **wife.**
He had found **happiness.**

I asked the students to get into groups of four and to underline all the nouns in the story. Next, they were to find three synonyms for each noun using the thesauruses and translation dictionaries in their mini-computers. We then created the following expanded story and I found a way to orchestrate the reading of it:

There was once a young **man**
A lad
An adolescent
A male

Who wanted to go on a **trip**
A voyage
A journey
An expedition

To a **country**
A land
A place
A nation

That would be exciting.

This young **man**
This lad
This adolescent
This male

Had the **idea**
The thought
The assumption
The concept

That the **world**
The universe

The globe
Human society

Would be more exciting than where he had once lived.
But he was wrong.

The **place**
The destination
The location
The space

Turned out to be a different in some ways and the same in others.

He had enjoyed his **time**
His visit
His interval
His limited period

In his new **country**
Land
Nation
Home

But the young **man**
The lad
The adolescent
The male

Returned to his **home**
His pied à terre
His place of birth
His locality

To live out the rest of his **life**
Time
Days
Existence

With his **wife**
Partner
Helpmeet
Lover

He had found **happiness**
Contentment
Gladness
Peace.

As a next step, I gave each group a chance to read their Four Times Story Nouns out loud. I numbered off each of the groups and assigned them a part to read out loud. They practiced for a few minutes. Then we read the story as a class. Each group of four was then asked to join another group with whom they shared their new vocabulary. We created a word wall, which we displayed in the classroom for the duration of the teachers' stay in Toronto. We added new vocabulary to the word wall as we worked together for eight weeks.

The following day, the students were more comfortable and more willing to participate in some drama exercises. They felt reassured that they had learned some new English vocabulary on one of their first days in Canada. I wanted to nudge them into trying something new—drama—by providing an opportunity for them to use some of their new vocabulary in a new kind of oral language context.

If Pictures Could Talk

I had prepared the first illustration in *The Arrival* as an overhead transparency. The illustration shows a man and a woman standing beside a kitchen table on which lies a closed suitcase. Both of the characters look sad and their hands touch on top of the suitcase. There are a teapot and two teacups in the foreground.

I asked the students to take a good, long look at the picture of the woman and the man with their hands touching. I asked them, "What do you think could be happening in this picture?" I then handed out the following template:

I see…

I remember…

I imagine…

I asked the teachers, working in groups of three, to view the illustration together and then write down all the elements that they could identify in it. By writing about what they saw, I was simply asking them to *decode* the picture. By asking them to write about what the picture reminded them of, I was asking them to *access prior knowledge*. And, finally, by asking them to imagine together what might be happening in the picture, I was asking them to *make inferences* in order to discover the meaning and the subtext in the picture.

Some of the teachers spoke in Chinese and wrote their answers in English. When they had finished filling out the template, we discussed their impressions of the picture. I helped them articulate their understandings. I asked them whether they were experiencing some of the feelings they had mentioned, such as sadness, anticipation, worry, and excitement. They nodded and smiled. One of the teachers said, "This really is us a few hours ago in another country—China. We have just come from this."

Next, I handed out a cutout thought bubble, a cutout speech bubble, and a square coloured sticky note. (A blackline master featuring a thought bubble, a speech bubble, and a whisper bubble appears at the back of this book.) Working in their groups, each teacher inferred what one of the characters was *thinking*, what the other character was *saying*, and what a *suitable caption* might be for the picture. The teachers then created minimalist scripts in which one teacher played the role of the narrator who read the caption; one teacher read the man's thoughts or words; and one teacher read the woman's thoughts or words.

Here are two examples of the work that the students created together:

CAPTION: THE TIME HAS COME
WOMAN (Thought bubble): I am going to miss him so much….
MAN: (Speech bubble): Please remember to write as often as you can….

CAPTION: THE FINAL FAREWELL
MAN (Thought bubble): She is strong and will be able to live on without me....
WOMAN: (Speech bubble): Your tea is growing cold....

Creating a Story Through Chamber Theatre

I asked for two volunteers—a man and a woman—to come to the front of the classroom and to recreate the scene in the picture. I asked them to "freeze" into an imitation of this image. I then asked for a volunteer group of three to come to the front of the classroom. The caption reader stood behind the couple. The person who had prepared the man's lines stood beside him. The person speaking the woman's lines stood beside her and spoke in role as that person—describing what the character was thinking and feeling.

The volunteers came to the front of the class. The caption reader announced:

THE TRIP TO FIND A LOST CHILD

The man with the thought bubble read these words out loud: "I am sorry to be leaving my wife but I am going to Canada to find my son. He left over three years ago and we have not heard from him. I will make the long journey to find him and to bring him back home." The female volunteer put her hand gently on the shoulder of the woman portraying the wife. Adopting the role of the wife, she spoke the words in her speech bubble, "Go, my husband, to find our son. I will wait for you forever."

Soon, we were immersed in creating a story to enhance oral language. The bonus was that what we were creating had connections to the Jiangsu teachers' own lives at that moment. Author Shaun Tan has this to say about the power of his picture book:

> In *The Arrival,* the absence of any written description also plants the reader more firmly in the shoes of an immigrant character. There is no guidance as to how the images might be interpreted, and we must ourselves search for meaning and seek familiarity in a world where such things are either scarce or concealed. Words have a remarkable magnetic pull on our attention, and how we interpret attendant images: in their absence, an image can often have more conceptual space around it, and invite a more lingering attention from a reader who might otherwise reach for the nearest convenient caption, and let that rule their imagination.

Kathleen Gallagher, Canada Research Chair in Urban School Research in Pegagogy and Policy at the Ontario Institute for Studies in Education, has encouraged me to do the kind of work in which students "make manifest their own subjectivities in the world evoked through character and play, a world laden with metaphor and nuance...." (2007) The teachers from Jiangsu became enamored with drama at the moment when they could see how the imagined contexts that they had created connected to the realities of their own lived experiences. The were delighted to be talking themselves into understanding—using new English vocabulary that affirmed their identities and allowed them to discover new things about themselves and the journey they had made to Canada.

In a Class of Her Own

As a teacher, I have always been interested in finding source material to link with dynamic instructional methods to pique the interest of my students. I am intent on making my classroom come alive with silent, shared, or guided reading, followed by discussion, argument, debate, laughter, and new insights. I find that motivating discouraged readers and writers to try to engage with text is made much more challenging because of the negative attitudes that struggling readers have developed toward print material. Some of them worry about the length of the reading passage as well as its difficulty. Deciphering the meaning behind the words is difficult, so I spend time tilling the ground—getting students ready psychologically as well as intellectually for the reading tasks that lie ahead.

In my experience, the introduction of graphic novels into a classroom has an electrifying effect no matter what the reading capacities of my students. There is something liberating and exciting about these books that feature such lively text and images. Students enjoy poring over graphic novels; they love the feel of them in their hands and in their pockets, and they are immediately drawn into the stories. They become intrigued by the images that help them bridge the gap between themselves and the text.

Developing Literacy Through Graphic Novels

Reading integrates a series of comprehension skills: questioning, visualizing, inferring, predicting, and making connections, to name but a few. With graphic novels, the scaffolding necessary to build solid readers lies in the architecture of the genre. There is evidence that the brain stores information not only verbally but also visually through dynamic mental images. Richly detailed images provide more potential for associative linking and more cognitive hooks that connect different bits of information in the reader's mind. The illustrations not only support the text—they are an integral part of the text. Students are given context clues within the subtle and sometimes not so subtle expressions, symbols, and actions of the characters within the story. Vocabulary is also supported within the illustrations and the text. The framework or grid layout of this text form lends itself perfectly to the strategy of predicting, a strategy needed to reach higher-level understanding in reading comprehension. The visual messages alongside the minimal print support the reader in processing the story by removing some of the obstacles presented by long passages of text.

One advantageous characteristic of graphic novels is that students can actually "see the fluency" that is required in reading a graphic novel. The big, bold print tells them to YELL or SCREAM. The whisper bubbles—a series of dotted lines—let them hear a different kind of emphasis. The flashback scenes are shaded differently. The thought bubbles help them see thinking come alive. In more traditional texts, some students have difficulty understanding when a character has "gone into his or her head" and is thinking about what is happening. Graphic novels help students understand that many different things are going on in a scene, and the visual nature of the texts allows them to view the action, perceive the thinking, immerse themselves in the setting or the landscape, and hear the dialogue.

Because pictures offer visual support for new vocabulary, graphic novels also help students who have difficulty visualizing. This text form is designed in such a way that the visuals help the reader see the important ideas so that they can infer meaning.

All of the following elements in a graphic novel work in combination with each other to help students read:

- Thought bubbles with text
- Speech bubbles with text
- Whisper bubbles with text
- Captions
- Symbols
- Sound effects
- Facial expressions
- Body language
- Landscape that sets a mood by means of lighting and color
- Action words with sounds and expressions

Graphic Novels and Teaching About Equity

I have written a number of graphic novels for elementary and secondary students and I found it challenging to limit the dialogue so as to allow the graphics to help students make meaning. One of my favorite experiences was writing a graphic novel about Ruby Bridges called *In a Class of Her Own* (published in 2006 by Scholastic Canada). It was a privilege to learn about Ruby's story and what she, her family, and others accomplished during the desegregation of schools in the American South in 1960.

Before I wrote the book, I did as much research as I could into Ruby's life, her family, the Civil Rights movement, and the 1954 U.S. Supreme Court ruling against "separate but equal" education. Even after I finished writing the book, I wanted to know more. And after working in classrooms with the book, I discovered that students also wanted to learn more about this courageous little girl and her family. The following outlines my typical approach to structuring lessons when I use *In a Class of Her Own* to teach students about equity issues.

1. Reading in Small Groups

The students work in groups of four and read the first chapter of the graphic novel out loud. I assign the following roles:

    Student 1: Caption reader
    Student 2: Ruby
    Student 3: Ruby's mother
    Student 4: Ruby's father

First, students do a "quick read" so they can figure out who is saying what. Then they do another reading that allows them to understand what is going on in the story.

2. Three Roles on the Wall

As a class, we draw two large outlines and one small outline of figures on large poster paper. One large figure represents Ruby's mother, the other Ruby's father. The small figure represents Ruby. I ask the students to decide which character they relate to the most. If they relate to the father, they stand on the left side of the classroom. If they relate to the mother, they stand on the right side of the classroom. If they relate to Ruby, they stand in the middle. (If you are worried about giving the students a choice, you can assign a role to them, although students usually choose the role assigned to them during the small-group read-aloud session.)

I ask for a volunteer from each of the groups and give each group a package of markers. Students stand near the appropriate figure that I have hung on the wall or put on a table. I ask the students to write adjectives that describe each character's feelings (e.g., anxious, worried, angry, scared, hopeful, proud) and to write those words on the *inside* of the figure. Next, I ask them to write character traits that describe each character (e.g., strong, brave, bitter, and so on). We then display the posters on the wall and study what has been created. We talk about the words that the students have chosen. I ask: "Who wrote the word *bitter* on the figure of the father? Why did you write that?" The student justifies his or her choice of words, for example, "The father is bitter because even though he won the Purple Heart in the army, he still faces discrimination at home."

3. Modeled Reading
As I read Chapter 2 to the class, students follow along with me. I sometimes ask for volunteer readers, but I rely upon the classroom teacher to let me know how to handle this.

4. Revisiting the Roles on the Wall
Once we have read the second chapter, which tells the story of Ruby's first day at school, we revisit the "Roles on the Wall." I appoint a recorder to write words that describe the *environment* that Ruby and her parents faced in New Orleans in 1960 on the *outside* of the figure. We write words such as *fear, prejudice, hatred, unfairness, violence, ignorance, police enforcement,* and so on.

I then ask the students: "Who and what do you suppose supported Ruby and her family as they made the decision to send her to school?" From the book, we know that Mrs. Henry was supportive, so we write her name *around* Ruby's figure to represent her support, but we need to do further research to find out who helped Ruby's family through this ordeal.

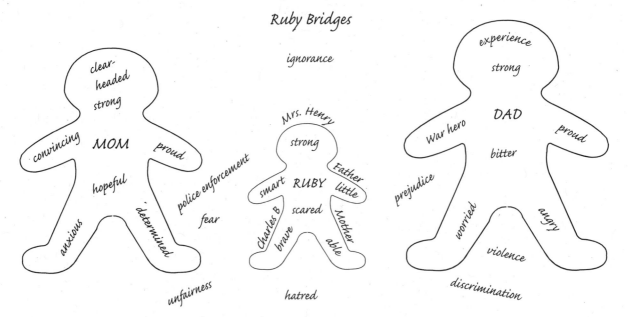

Roles on the Wall

Ruby Bridges

Examples for further research include:

Ruby's Father
Ruby's Family
Charles Burk, one of the United States marshals who walked Ruby into the school every morning
Robert Coles, the psychiatrist who was assigned to help Ruby cope with her ordeal

5. Reading in Small Groups
We then read Chapter 3 in small groups.

Student 1: Caption reader and sign reader
Student 2: Ruby
Student 3: Mrs. Henry
Student 4: Caretaker
Student 5: All others

Once again, I have the students do a quick read and then go back to read for meaning.

6. Bursting the Bubble
This chapter elaborates on Ruby's feelings during her ordeal. On the last page of the chapter we "burst the bubbles" of each of the characters. I ask the students to choose one of the characters and to write the words from their speech bubble at the top of a page. Then I ask them, "If we could burst the bubbles of each of these characters and have them tell us more about what they are going through, what would they say?" They then write more about what that character might say or think.

When students write their final draft, they cut the paper to make it look like a speech bubble, a whisper bubble, or a thought bubble, as shown below. Ruby tells her story— about how she thought she might be poisoned. Mrs. Henry tells her story of what it is like to teach in a school where her own colleagues will have nothing to do with her. The caretaker has witnessed a lot in his lifetime but this little girl's suffering has really affected him. He tells his story about what he sees every day when Ruby comes to school.

MRS. HENRY:
Look at what this poor child has gone through. There is so much hatred in the world. Ruby is a survivor—that's what she is. What I have to put up with in the staffroom is nothing to what she has to go through every day on her way to school. This child is remarkable in every way.

CARETAKER:
I watch Ruby every day coming to school with her mother. She always stands so tall and looks so serious. I see her mother's worried face and I feel so much sadness that the world has to treat people this way. The poor kid. No lunch for months and months. This will take some cleaning but it's the least I can do for little Ruby.

RUBY:
Momma always packs me a lunch. I see her put everything in a bag and she always gives it to me as I enter the classroom. But I haven't had lunch for about two months. I keep seeing the sign that said that they are going to poison me. I believe them. So I hide my lunch. I never thought that it would smell like it did. I am so sorry that I lied to everyone, especially Mrs. Henry who is so good to me. I was just afraid.

7. Inner/Outer Circle: Reading Our Writing

Inner/outer circle reading allows students to discover how elements of their writing can be juxtaposed to create a theatrical reading representing various perspectives. Here is how I set this up:

Once all group members complete their writing, I position them one group at a time in the center of the classroom. I ask the students who have written as Mrs. Henry to sit on chairs and the students who have written as Ruby to sit at their feet. The caretakers stand behind Mrs. Henry's chair. As the orchestra leader, I give these directions: "When I touch you gently on the shoulder, I want you to begin reading your writing. As soon as you hear another person reading, you stop and listen to the next voice. If I touch your shoulder again, it means that I want you to continue reading from where you left off. In this way we will be creating a combination of viewpoints and voices that will tell more of Ruby Bridge's story in a moving, theatrical way."

Here is a transcript of what an inner/outer circle reading might look like:

> RUBY:
> Momma always packs me a lunch. I see her put everything in a bag and she always gives it to me as I enter the classroom.
> MRS. HENRY:
> Look at what this poor child has gone through. There is so much hatred in the world. Ruby is a survivor—that's what she is.
> CARETAKER:
> I watch Ruby every day coming to school with her mother. She always stands so tall and looks so serious.
> RUBY:
> Why are people so mean? Why can't they…?
> CARETAKER:
> Although sometimes I do see a twinkle in her eye.
> RUBY:
> Peanut butter sandwiches, I love them
> CARETAKER:
> I don't know whether I could put my children through something like this.
> RUBY:
> I have not eaten a lunch for two months.
> MRS. HENRY:
> Ruby is a remarkable girl.

Ruby Bridge's sacrifices and the risk-laden choices that she and her family made are an inspiration to everyone. Jonas, the fictional protagonist in Lois Lowry's brilliant novel, *The Giver*, also makes a difficult personal choice—to save the baby Gabriel from being released from the community. Jonas decides to escape the only world that he has known and he takes the baby with him into the unknown world of Elsewhere. The next section explores the themes of freedom of choice and freedom from oppression.

The Giver

> We must take sides. Neutrality helps the oppressor, never the victim. Silence encourages the tormentor, never the tormented. Sometimes we must interfere.
>
> Elie Weisel

The protagonist in Lois Lowry's novel *The Giver* is named Jonas. When Jonas is 12 years old, he is chosen to be the community's Receiver of Memories. He enters into training with an elderly man called The Giver. From The Giver, Jonas learns about pain, sadness, war, and all the unhappy truths of the "real" world. He gradually realizes that the community in which he lives is controlled and unnatural. *The Giver* presents a "today" world of sameness: no yesterdays, no differentiated human rights, and no opportunity for anyone to exercise the freedom to think critically or imaginatively: "Jonas lives in a community that was so meticulously ordered, the choices so carefully made" (*The Giver*, p. 48).

Map-Making

When I worked with a Grade 7 class who had read the first few chapters of the book, I asked the students to create a map of Jonas's community. We brainstormed a list of the places that they had read about in the novel: the Nurturing Center, the Auditorium, the Central Plaza, the Childcare Center, the Food Distribution Center, the Birthing Center, the House of the Old, the Hall of the Open Records, the Food Production Center, and the Department of Justice.

I asked the students to get into groups of six. They were to re-create the environment of the novel by constructing a map that would help us "see" the way in which the society was laid out. The groups could add other things that they had noticed in the book as well, for example, the waste reduction centre and the horticulture centre. Once the maps were completed, the groups shared them with one another.

I believe that I am on the earth to comfort the afflicted but just as importantly to afflict the comfortable.

John Murrell

Making Lists

As a next step, I invited the students to put on their skeptics' hats. I asked them, "If you lived in this community, what places would you avoid? Why? What would make you feel uneasy? What would you question almost immediately? Let your uneasiness be your guide and circle the places on the map that you might avoid."

Referring to the maps, the students talked about which places made them uneasy. They talked about the Birthing Center in particular and how women who gave birth to babies were looked down upon in this society. We then moved on to create a list of our fears and uneasiness based on our reading of the beginning chapters:

1. Fear of being released from the community
2. Having to make an apology to the class if you were late
3. Having to disclose feelings to your parents and siblings every evening in the telling of feelings time
4. Not having a choice about your future beyond the age of twelve

5. Being controlled in every way: birth, nurturing, thinking
6. Having to obey the rules even if they don't make sense
7. Knowing that imperfect babies, the old, and the sick are "released"
8. Not being able to question the way that things are done
9. Taking pills to squash sexual feelings
10. Not knowing what lies beyond the community

Critical Questioning

As a class, we brainstormed ten critical questions for which we had no answers:

1. When people are released, where do they go?
2. What happens to them?
3. What is "Elsewhere" like?
4. Do people live or die there after they are released?
5. How is Jonas's society scrutinized? Are there cameras all around? Are homes bugged with microphones?
6. Where are the security guards stationed?
7. Are there loudspeakers on poles throughout the community?
8. Who really is in charge?
9. Does everybody think this is a good way to live?
10. Does the outside world know about Jonas's world?

Each group then created a list of 20 categories of groups or individuals that are mentioned in the book:

1. Committee of elders
2. Security guards
3. Birth mothers
4. Sanitation laborer
5. Teachers
6. Nurturers
7. Doctors
8. Engineers
9. Caretaker/Recreation Director in the House of the Old
10. Assistant Director of Recreation
11. Street cleaners
12. Landscape workers
13. Laborers
14. Pilots
15. Lawyers in the Department of Justice
16. Fish hatchery attendant
17. Maintenance crews
18. Department of bicycle repair
19. Distributor of the pills that stop the urgings
20. Hair ribbon cutter and distributor

Interviewing in Role

I asked the students to get into small groups. I asked for one volunteer from each group to play one of the roles on the list that we had generated. They spent a moment studying the list and then told their group members the role they had chosen. One girl decided to be the Distributor of the pills that stop the urgings; another chose to be a birth mother; two boys chose to be pilots; another student chose to be the Recreation Director in the House of the Old. Another chose to be a security guard.

The volunteers went into the hallway of the school with the classroom teacher. The groups that were left in the classroom were told that they were going to role-play the members of the Advisory Committee Looking into the Release of Individuals. Every few months, this committee conducts random interviews of people to make sure that they are obeying the rules. The interview that they would be conducting would ensure that their society is functioning properly.

The committee members were instructed to devise a list of interview questions to ask each volunteer in role. The answers to these questions would either satisfy them that the individual worker was doing his or her job—or not. The questions could be either general or specific.

The volunteers in the hallways, who had all chosen a specific role, were to decide on their name, the place where they worked, and their life history. Then they were asked to fill out the following questionnaire:

> Name:
> Age:
> Marital status:
> Number of children assigned to your dwelling:
> Place of Work:
> Duties at work:
> Problems in the workplace:
> Problems in the home:
> Are your feelings always under control?   YES   NO
>   (Circle one, please)
> Do you have any questions for the committee? Please list them on the back of the sheet.

The class ended. I made enough copies of the questionnaire and the list of questions for each committee member. I asked the students not to reveal what had been written.

The next day, after the class was settled in their groups, I asked the volunteers to come to the front of the classroom. They were to introduce themselves and their role to the class. While they were preparing what they would say, I asked each group to select a chairperson of the committee. I handed each chairperson the questionnaire that the group had created containing the list of questions. After each volunteer had introduced him- or herself, I directed them to their group and asked the chairperson to stand. Before I gave the signal for the interviews to begin, I reminded the students that they would be expected to do the following:

- Maintain their role and keep the role-playing going.
- Maintain seriousness of purpose.
- Avoid sabotaging the group's efforts.
- Listen carefully and work from each other's answers.
- Be respectful and sustain their belief in the drama.

I gave the signal and the interviews began. I wandered through the classroom listening to the students improvising in role.

Questioning in Role

After about 15 minutes, I stopped the role-playing and interviewed both the committee members and the workers in role. I posed the following questions:

To the individual being interviewed:
What is your name?
What is the nature of your work?
Have you ever been interviewed by this committee before?
How comfortable were you during the interview?
What do you think was the purpose of the interview?
Do you think that you made a positive or negative impression? Why or why not?
As you left the interview, what were your overall feelings?

To the members of the Advisory Committee Looking into the Release of Individuals, I asked the following questions:
What was your overall impression of this worker?
Did the individual answer your questions to your satisfaction?
What questions posed some difficulty for him or her?
Why were you suspicious of this person in the first place?
Will you be recommending this person's release from the community? Why or why not?

Writing in Role

I then asked each committee member to write a formal report about the findings of the Advisory Committee Looking into the Release of Individuals, and the person who was interviewed wrote a secret diary entry. Here are some samples of students' writing:

Committee member's report:
The committee and I met with a strange little man called Samuel today who is a Sanitation Worker. He works the night shift and the reason that we called him in is that he has been late to work numerous times. We had him checked out by the doctor who has prescribed energy boosters. He actually told us that he did not really like his job and that he was not comfortable taking the energy boosters because he was not sure what was in them. We did not like his questioning attitude, AT ALL. We will be putting hidden cameras in the kitchen of his dwelling and will be observing him 24/7. If we don't like what we see in the next few days, there really is only one solution to our dilemma. Farewell, Samuel!

A birth mother's secret diary entry:
Dear diary,
They treated me with such disrespect in the interview. I wasn't even allowed to sit on a chair and they asked me so many questions that I did not know the answers to. I am thinking of running away. I have thought about it for a long time now but it is complicated. I have just given birth and need to be with the

baby for the next few months. But then they will take this baby away and it will be easier to run.

Out-of-Role Reflection

The class discussion after the role-playing was electrifying. The students were beginning to understand just how overly controlled and scary Jonas's world really was. One student talked about how the committee members had all been terribly polite but there was a sinister quality to their questions. He felt that there was a "trick" of some kind going on that he could not figure out.

We then began to discuss how everybody and everything in the book looks so perfect at first. Some students began to recognize the dark undercurrents in the book, but they only did so after the role-playing exercise. I told them that this was probably author Lois Lowry's intention and I read aloud something that Lowry had written about her book:

> When Jonas meets The Giver for the first time, and tries to comprehend what lies before him, he says in confusion, "I thought there was only us. I thought there was only now."
>
> In the beginning to write The Giver, I created, as I always do, in every book, a world that existed only in my imagination—the world of "only us, only now." I tried to make Jonas's world seem familiar, comfortable, and safe, and I tried to seduce the reader. I seduced myself along the way. It did feel good, that world. I got rid of all the things that I fear and dislike: all the violence, prejudice, poverty, and injustice; and I even threw in good manners as a way of life because I liked the idea of it. One child has pointed out, in a letter, that the people in Jonas's world didn't even have to do dishes. It was very, very tempting to leave it at that. But I've never been a writer of fairy tales. And if I've learned anything through that river of memories, it is that we can't live in a walled world, in an "only us, only now" world, where we are all the same and feel safe. We would have to sacrifice too much. The richness and color would disappear. Feelings for other human beings would no longer be necessary. Choice would be obsolete.

Being oppressed means the absence of choices.

bell hooks

We then began to examine how important it is to have choice—and to know that one always has a choice to do good or evil. The students were now eager and prepared to continue learning about Jonas and the difficult choice he would have to make later in the novel.

It is up to us as teachers to instill in our students an attitude of healthy skepticism and critical literacy and to give them safe opportunities to engage in discussions about the uncertainty in the world. This lesson allowed students to explore what it must be like to live without freedom in order to understand how important and precious freedom is.

Nobody Rides the Unicorn

I once worked in a Grade 4 classroom in which there were a large number of students with special needs as well as a number of English Language Learners. The school's main focus for the year was on vocabulary building. I thought that *Nobody Rides a Unicorn* would be a good source to help students become critically aware of the power of words and how words can be used for good or for evil. In the three mornings that I would spend with the class, I anticipated having the students learn to explore how they could use their bodies to interpret the nuances of word meanings.

From the moment I entered the classroom with the book under my arm, it was obvious that the students were excited about having a guest who would read to them. They told me that they loved stories and that their teacher read to them many times a day. They settled quietly on the carpet. I explained to them that we would be spending time together looking at the pictures and the words in the picture book I had brought—discovering how words and pictures work together and exploring how the author used certain words deliberately in order to draw readers into the story.

Before Reading

We began by looking at the cover of the book and talking about unicorns. We recorded what students already knew about unicorns on a flip chart:

- Unicorns are magical.
- They look like a horse but they have a horn.
- They make me sad for some reason.
- They don't really exist.
- They are found in myths and legends.
- They usually do good not evil.

One girl who was an avid reader thought a unicorn's horn could neutralize poison. I was impressed that she knew the word "neutralize" and I helped the rest of the students understand the meaning of this word. As I recorded the students' ideas on the chalkboard, something incredible happened. One boy pointed to another boy's pullover and said, "Look. Stephen is wearing a unicorn". And sure enough, Stephen was wearing a pullover that his grandmother had brought him from England just days before. In the image on the front of the pullover, two unicorns supported the royal Scottish coat-of-arms, while a lion and a unicorn supported the coat-of-arms of the United Kingdom. Stephen stood up so we could examine the unicorns in detail and he seemed thrilled by the attention. According to the classroom teacher, Stephen was a very quiet and shy child. But for the first time he was the center of attention and he didn't seem to mind at all. I didn't mind either! I am always thrilled by" teachable moments" and I urge my student teachers to be open to the surprise and delight that comes when students connect to source material in unexpected ways. Stephen's pullover allowed the students to find personal meaning in what we were learning and it provided an auspicious entry point for me as the teacher.

During Reading

We returned to the picture book and tried to understand what the title meant. Here were some of the students' speculations: "Maybe the unicorn is special so they have had to make rules to make sure that nobody rides him and hurts him." "Maybe he doesn't like to be ridden." "Maybe he is magical and something happens to the rider if she rides him." I then began to read the story:

In a faraway land of Joppardy there was once a king who was full of fear. He was afraid of everybody in the world. He was sure they were plotting to put poison in his wine or his food. So the king called the most cunning man in Joppardy, a man named Doctor Slythe.

I stopped reading and we studied the pictures. I asked the students why they thought such a powerful king would be so afraid? I asked the students if they knew what the word "cunning" meant. They were able to infer that it meant something similar to the word "mean." We looked up the word in a dictionary. I wrote the following definitions on the board: *cunning = crafty, deceiving, sly, secretive, mischievous.*

Making Predictions

I circled the word *sly* on the board. The students noticed that Dr. Slythe's name contained this word. I asked them to predict what they thought Dr. Slythe might look like:

- What do you think he wears during the day?
- What do you predict his nose looks like?
- What do you imagine he wears on his head? On his hands?
- Do you predict that he might have a beard or a moustache?

Based on the students' responses, I wrote this descriptive paragraph on the chalkboard using the vocabulary that the students had offered while augmenting it with some words of my own:

Dr. Slythe is a very tall man. He wears a large black cloak that covers most of his body. He has a red carnation in the lapel of his coat. He has a long nose with a wart on the end of it. He wears a large hat with a wide brim that covers his eyes. He always wears gloves so that he does not leave fingerprints on anything that he touches. He has a dark moustache that hides his mouth and makes him look frightening.

We read our writing in unison as a class. I then asked the students if they wished to see how the book's illustrator, Stephen Lambert, had drawn Dr. Slythe. I turned the page and there was the picture. I asked the students to think about what we had been able to create in our imaginations by simply knowing the word *sly*. Our predictions were correct except for the nose and the gloves—but we had captured the essence of the character quite well.

I continued reading the story. Dr. Slythe tells the King that the only way to avoid being poisoned is to drink from a goblet made of a unicorn's horn and to eat with a knife, fork, and spoon that were also made from a unicorn's horn. "The unicorn can only be trapped by a quiet young girl with a gentle voice," advises Dr. Slythe. Zoë is the young girl with the gentle voice whom the King and Dr. Slythe approach to find the unicorn. She is brought before the king and Doctor Slythe tells her that they will take her deep into the forest. There she will sit alone and sing until a unicorn appears and lays his head in her lap.

Voices in the Head

I asked the students if they thought that Zoë should honor the King's wishes. Their responses varied. I asked them to form two lines in the classroom. One student volunteered to play Zoë. I told the students to pretend to be the voices in Zoe's head. They could give her advice about what to do. The students lined up. As the volunteer playing Zoë walked down the aisle, the students whispered their advice to her:

"Don't go. You should not trust anyone called Dr. Slythe."
"Take a friend with you. Do not go alone."
"As soon as the unicorn comes to you, run away."
"This king and his advisor are lying."

When the student playing Zoë reached the end of the line, I asked her what she had decided to do. She said that she would refuse to go into the forest. We sat down as a class and I said, "If Zoë decides to disobey the King's orders, what will become of her? She is nobody's child and she will not survive. She is totally alone in the world."

We read on. Sure enough, Zoë was duped into trusting the king and the unicorn was wounded, captured, and led away to the King's palace.

Brainstorming

In groups, the students wrote out an action plan for what Zoë could do now. I gave them large sheets of paper and they recorded their ideas in point form. We shared these ideas as a class, for example:

- Zoë and the unicorn should stay away from the castle forever.
- Zoë should build a wall so that the King and Dr. Slythe will never find her.

I then read the rest of the story, which describes how Zoë manages to free the unicorn and is eventually reunited with the animal in his magical world.

Nobody Rides the Unicorn allowed the students to talk about bullying in a safe way. I also wanted to provide the children with an experience that allowed them to question what people in authority say and how they say it. I hoped that they would understand how powerful words are. I wanted them to deduce from the story the fact that they should not believe everything they hear or see and that it is important to develop critical thinking skills.

Encounter

Pedagogy in the critical sense illuminates the relationship among knowledge, authority, and power.

Henry Giroux

I want to equip all my students with the thinking skills and tools they need to critically analyze information that they gather in school, on the Internet, in discussions with friends and acquaintances, and in the media. I want them to become sensitive to the ways in which race, ethnicity, gender, class, sexuality, and other identifiers are represented in the stories that they read. Through the work that we do together in the classroom, I hope that they come to view all the information they gather with a discriminating eye and become conscious of alternative perspectives and alternative histories.

When I am invited into classrooms to do work in history and drama, I usually begin by talking about how history has been constructed. Whose stories are being told? What stories are clamoring to be told but have been silenced? What conditions were in place that made the tellers of these stories invisible? How has the way that we have been taught about difference divided us? In his book

Learning to Divide the World: Education at Empire's End (1998), John Willinsky helped me to see that we must not only teach students literature and history that depicts personal struggles against discrimination, but we must also give students a sense of how English literature and the way that history has been constructed "was used to teach people their distance from the center of civilization":

> Schools have offered students little help in fathoming why this sense of difference in race, culture, and nation is so closely woven into the fabric of society. As a result, students have been relatively unaware of such government measures as the racial restriction of access to voting, immigration, and public services until not so long ago. They need to see that such divisions have long been part of the fabric and structure of the state, including the schools, and they need to appreciate that challenging the structuring of those differences requires equally public acts of refusing their original and intended meanings.

Glenys McQueen Fuentes is a professor of Theatre Studies at Brock University in Ontario. Glenys and I have worked together on many occasions with teachers of elementary or secondary students, using drama and movement to uncover hidden truths in a wide variety of material, including myths, poetry, novels, and picture books. We once worked with a group of Grade 7 and 8 students who were about to embark on a theme-based unit on colonization using Jane Yolen's picture book *Encounter*.

Glenys and I decided to use Glenys's strategy of hieroglyphics in our teaching. We wanted the students to create a myth, story, or message inspired by their interpretation of the following series of symbols:

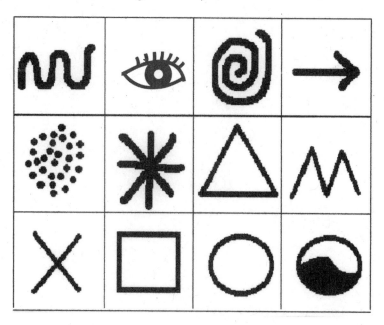

We divided the class into groups of five. We asked them to pretend that they were the last members of an ancient civilization that had developed sophisticated cultural symbols, myths, and legends. They were the last of their people because the rest of their society had died from illness, had been killed by conquerors, or had disappeared for unknown reasons. Therefore, these people wanted to leave a final mark to record their existence. We asked the students to answer the following questions:

- How old is your civilization?
- In what part of the world do you live?
- How do you survive day by day?
- Who are the most revered members of your civilization, and why?
- What objects and ideas are important in your culture?

We handed each group an envelope containing the symbols cut up into squares.

We asked the students to collaborate in their groups to create and record an important cultural story, myth, or message by arranging their symbols in an order that made sense to them. The story, myth, or message was to represent the essence of their civilization and they must record it as faithfully as possible.

The students opened the envelopes and laid out the symbols. They worked for about 20 minutes arranging the symbols so that they communicated a meaning. We encouraged the students to verbalize the message or myth first and then find a way to represent it with their symbols. We asked that they pay attention to the meaning and the patterning of the symbols as they positioned them in juxtaposition to each other. We reminded them that the arrangement of the pattern was an important part of the message.

Interpreting the Story, Myth, or Message

Next, we asked each group to figure out a way to use the symbols as the basis of a movement exploration. The students were to create what Glenys calls "instant choreography" by interpreting the symbols through movement. Initially, Glenys showed the whole class how to experiment with qualities of movement (fast, slow, jagged, straight); levels (high, medium, low); pathways (how far can we move across the room?); and movements in unison as well as individualized movements. Then we brought the students back into their groups and they practiced their interpretations. We played music to enhance the choreography. The music added a dimension that seemed to bind the students to their story, myth, or message. They were not only connected to it physically and intellectually; they were connected to it emotionally as well.

Deciphering the Story, Myth, or Message

We then asked the students to move away from their cultural symbols and to stand against the classroom wall. It struck us that some students were clearly reluctant to leave their message behind, and some went back to check that the pattern of their symbols was undisturbed.

Now came the challenging part of the lesson. We asked that the groups move clockwise, so that they were in front of another group's symbol pattern. We invited each group to interpret the new story, myth, or message that lay before them, whose pattern was quite different from the pattern they had left behind just minutes before.

We asked each group to appoint a recorder. The recorder wrote down the group's interpretation of the story, myth, or message as students in each group answered the following questions:

…what we choose to tell, to whom we choose to tell it, and indeed, how we choose to tell it, all matter.

Belarie Zatzman

- What do you think this new pattern means?
- Why do you think it was created this way?
- How is the pattern different/similar compared to your group's pattern?

We brought the groups back together. Each group shared their original choreography with the other group and then shared their story, myth, or message. The visiting group read their interpretation to the other group. The groups compared interpretations.

Evaluation

In the discussion that followed, we posed these questions:

- What was it like to think of others interpreting your symbolic pattern?
- Were you worried that your story, myth, or message would not be fully understood?
- How did your group view the second pattern? Was it hard to forget your own, original interpretation?
- Did the fact that you had left your own pattern behind make any difference in how you reacted to the second pattern?
- Have you ever had to change neighborhoods? schools? countries? languages? customs? How challenging is it for people to understand other people's traditions, families, cultures, and languages?
- Has there ever been a time when something that mattered to you a great deal was taken from you unfairly?
- What is it like to be misunderstood by people who don't really know you? What are the feelings associated with being misunderstood?
- Can you think of historical exoduses, disappearances, and examples of cultural messages left behind in different parts of the world? in different forms?
- What have you thought about since doing this exercise?

Brainstorming

The next day, I wrote the word "premonition" on the chalkboard and I asked the students what they thought the word meant. Here is a sampling of their answers:

- A warning about something that is going to happen
- A gut feeling about the future
- Something in the future that comes through your subconscious
- Sometimes a premonition comes to you in a dream or a daydream

Reading Out Loud

I told the students that I was going to read them a story about a boy who had a premonition of things to come. I read them Jane Yolen's book *Encounter.*
After reading the story, I said: "The young boy had a premonition about what was going to happen to his community. No one listened to him. Why did the chief not listen to the boy? What was the result of his unresponsiveness to the boy's anxiety?"

I asked the students to form groups of six. I asked for one volunteer from each group to come to the front of the classroom. The volunteer was to play the role of the boy who had had the dream about the strangers. Each group was to play a different group of people:

Group 1: members of the boy's family
Group 2: the Elders of the tribe, including the chief
Group 3: the boy's friends
Group 4: the healers in the community
Group 5: the boy's teachers
Group 6: the community's religious leaders

I asked each group to think of possible reasons for not listening or believing the boy and the kind of strategy that they would use when he came to tell them his story. I asked each student role-playing the boy to go back to his group. On my signal, he was to begin telling the story of his premonition or dream to the group. The group would respond. On my signal, the boys would go to another group to try to tell their story. The exercise would continue until every boy had told the story to every group.

We began the role-play. The group playing the family made fun of the boy's dream. "You are always coming up with these crazy ideas," scoffed the boy's mother. The friends refused to listen to the boy. The Elders were understanding at first but then became impatient. The healers questioned the boy's sanity, the religious leaders questioned his faith, and the teachers threatened the boy with punishment.

Reflection

After the role-playing exercise, I invited all the students who had played the boy to sit on chairs at the front of the classroom. I asked them to describe what it was like to pretend to be the boy in the story. At first there was a lot of laughter as they recounted what had happened, but then the discussion became more serious and they talked about how the world might have been very different if the boy had been able to make the Elders listen. We talked about how frustrating it is when powerful people do not believe the stories that we tell. The conversation drifted to a girl's desire for her mother to stop smoking, and to an encounter that a student had had with the police in which he was accused of something that he had not done. How true was this ancient story, they wanted to know?

I handed out an adapted version of Christopher Columbus's diary and we compared notes.

Revisiting the Dream

As a culminating activity, I asked the students to imagine that the boy is one of the people that Christopher Columbus takes back with him to the court in Spain. He has a dream the night before he sails with the others—in which he has a premonition of things to come. I asked the students to describe the dream in role, incorporating words from Columbus's diary as well as ideas of their own that had emerged as they worked with their peers on this unit.

Here is one example of the writing produced by a Grade 7 student in response to this excerpt from Columbus's diary: *"If it please our Lord, I intend at my return to carry home six of them to your Highnesses, that they may learn our language."* (The student's name has been changed to ensure privacy.)

I don't want to learn their languages or dress in their clothes, or eat their food, or be with them at all. I told the chief that if I was one of the ones chosen from our island to go on the voyage tomorrow I would run away. I will dive into the sea and swim until death overtakes me.

Last night I had another dream—this one more frightening than the last one. I dreamt of their eyes that are the colour of a muddy river... eyes that stare and stare and stare. Greedy eyes. Eyes that want something from me but I am not sure what. Eyes that make me not see myself as I truly am.

I woke up. I begged my mother to hide me. She wanted to but knew that the chief would find me. If I can't make my own family understand the mistakes that they are making, how can I make these strangers see that they are destroying something more precious than life?

So it was that we lost our lands to the strangers from the sky.

Ephraim Grade 7

In the following letter, Glenys reminded me of another occasion on which we had carried out the story/myth/message exercise in the library of a Toronto school with a group of Grade 5 students. The outcome was slightly different but still very powerful:

As the work came to a close (they were told they had one minute to finish), I asked them to stand and look one last time at their message. They were directed to turn their backs on their message. This moment represented their having to leave their message and their lands. Then, as they walked (still in their groups) clockwise toward the next group's image, they were to imagine that 1000 years had passed, and that they were the descendants of those original people. They had heard the story as it passed from generation to generation. They were to imagine that they were returning to the lands of their ancestors to try and find the original message. As they arrived at the next group's area, where the message had been left, they were to look at it carefully. Perhaps it would be different than they had imagined ... much time had passed.

To here, all went as per usual—the students were engaged and took to the translating with little problem. However, as the groups began to move, there was one group of little boys, who had been particularly active and engaged in the "translation" activity. They were clearly anxious and were unwilling to leave their message behind. When urged to do so, their anxiety level rose considerably and they simply could not contain themselves (they had been asked to move in silence). They literally blurted out: "But what if the next group ruins our message? What if they don't see it? What if they don't understand it? What if they read it wrong?" They were absolutely unable to "go on" with worry over it.

My recollection was that at that moment, we stopped everyone and let the group of boys return to their original pattern, so they could warn their "descendants" about where the message was and why it was so important to be extremely careful with it. At that point, we understood their worry. With GREAT pride, they showed us that they had placed their message VERY carefully under a desk, in a corner of the room. The location had been chosen to keep the message safe from weather and people who, not recognizing its significance, might wreck, alter or ruin it. What was even more impressive was

HOW they had constructed their message. As the half-file cards were made of cardboard, they had created a 2-storey "house of cards" effect—with the symbols on the inside! This, too, had been done to ensure it would be hidden and that there would be less chance of random violence against it. It was absolutely amazing—no wonder they were worried about it. The logic, ingenuity, thought processes, care and skill which they put into it was extraordinary, and very clear....

This moment simply had to be the centre of the entire afternoon. Although we had planned on taking the workshop several steps further, and ending with a movement/ritual version of each group's "found" legend, the boys had created a gigantic panorama for reflection. The other groups each began to talk of the time and energy they had taken with their messages. Several students in other groups confessed to also worrying that the next group might mess up their work, or not understand what they had said, or ruin their very important message. It became a reflection on these fears and others. This jumped into a conversation about how important it is that our "messages" be understood ... and how difficult it was when we were misunderstood, how easy that is, compared to the difficulty of "creating" a message. It went seamlessly into talk of perceptions, misconceptions, being "different," being in new lands and in new cultures and languages, of how we do not see the richness of things left behind, and no one else may understand that. It also became a discussion of how important it is to reflect on what others are trying to "say," on how we may only see part of the message, on being careful of and understanding of others, who are having difficulty being heard or understood, etc. I think it was by far the most extraordinary experience with the hieroglyphics that I've had—before or after!

5

Interpreting Text Through Active Engagement (Secondary)

> I have learned two lessons in my life: first, there are no sufficient literary, psychological, or historical answers to human tragedy, only moral ones. Second, just as despair can come to one another only from other human beings, hope, too, can be given to one only by other human beings.
> —Elie Wiesel

To do the kind of work in drama that I perform in schools, I strive to create communities of caring in which we move beyond estrangement and alienation. Through drama and other interactive exercises, I try very hard to establish "classrooms of conscience" in which students feel safe to talk about difficult issues, take responsibility for their decisions, and feel empowered to make the world a better place for everyone. I want my students not only to recognize injustice but also to develop an understanding and appreciation of what it means to struggle for the sake of justice.

In 2007, my Chinese students from Jiangsu province and I were invited to attend the Ontario Education Leadership Centre near Orillia, Ontario. After traveling from Toronto by bus to the Centre, the Chinese students participated in a workshop with me and a group of Rama Anishinabe students from Mnjikaning Kendaaswin (*"Place of Learning"*) Elementary School. We titled our workshop "This Land is Your Land, This Land is My Land?" Through movement and song, the Rama Anishinabe students told the story of how Europeans came to the New World and took the lands that once belonged to First Nations peoples. As they re-enacted what it must have been like to witness their ancestors' civilizations crumble, I asked each Anishinabe student to express "a warning that they held in their hearts and advice that they held in their minds." Here are some examples of what the students said:

Warnings

- Do not make assumptions about us, for example, that Anishinabe people are less intelligent than white people.
- Do not take our children away to residential schools. [This statement was made just days after June 11, 2008, the date on which the Canadian

government issued an apology to Canada's Aboriginal peoples for the damage to First Nations families caused by residential schools.]

- Do not poison our rivers.
- Do not kill so many animals in the forest that they become extinct.

Advice

- Learn about us.
- Learn from us—we know the ways of nature.
- Don't believe the lies that tell you that we are savages.
- Do not tell us lies.
- Do not trick us.

The workshop was intense and emotional. The Chinese students were overwhelmed by the experiences that the Anishinabe students shared with them. Marsha, an Anishinabe teacher candidate who had worked with the students for many months teaching them about their heritage, had obviously made a huge impact. The elementary students saw in Marsha a strong role model who had taken risks in her teaching and who had led them to a place where they were now the teachers telling an essential story. Marsha wrote the following note to me and to Judy Blaney, her course director, who had supported Marsha throughout the entire year in her work with this particular class:

> Dear Kathy and Judy:
> Thank you so much and Chi Miigwech (a Big Thanks!!) for asking me to be part of your day in hosting the teachers from China. I was a little apprehensive at first, drama not being one of my strong points, but having both of you behind me gave me the courage to see it through. Having the girls there really gave it that special touch to what it means to be Aboriginal. I can see that they have already overcome some of those barriers about not being shy and being proud about who they are. I am honored that you included me and would be happy to work with you both again.
>
> Once again, thank you.
> Marsha

Residential Schools: The Stolen Years

I am privileged to teach a course at York University called "Teaching Social Studies through the Arts." My colleagues and I developed a series of lessons to help intermediate and senior students learn about the societal and psychological impact of residential schools on Aboriginal communities.

I use artifacts a lot in my teaching in general, but especially when teaching social studies. I search for artifacts in antique stores, galleries, and other such places and I keep them in an old suitcase that also comes in handy in various teaching situations. I have gathered a bunch of old keys, a number of colorful scarves, an assortment of old photographs, maps, the collar of a dress, an antique puppet that is crumpled and disheveled, stones with symbols on them, a clown's make-up kit, a hat pin, an old perfume bottle, a collection of old letters, and a diary that my great-uncle wrote during the First World War. I use these artifacts in all sorts of ways as I design my lessons. The artifacts are introduced at specific points to "hook" students into wondering about the items and to prompt them to ask questions. I use artifacts to introduce historical events, picture books, and new concepts, to help students navigate difficult texts and discover connections in common with their classmates, and to inspire discussion and debate. Students love the fact that they are allowed to touch the materials, pass them around a circle in small groups, wonder about their use or origin, link them to the characters and incidents in the books and poetry they are reading, and use them in their oral presentations to the class.

As I introduced my first lesson on residential schools, I asked my student teachers to find a partner. I asked them to decide who would be A and who would be B. I handed each of them a primary source excerpt from a book called *Residential Schools: The Stolen Years* (ed. Linda Jaine, 1993). Each pair of students read the following primary source material—two monologues—and talked to each other about what it might have felt like to be wrenched away from one's home and family.

> From the day my mother walked my brother, sisters and I up to that ominously looming structure, I began to understand the depth of those black-robe's power and influence. Almost immediately my mother's authority was undermined and subverted by a nun who authoritatively pushed her out the door and warned her not to get emotional about saying goodbye.
>
> While I cried and fiercely clung to one of my sisters the nun ran through the rules which I never seemed to remember and was consequently punished for, and quickly was showed the rest of the school.
>
> Soon after, I was torn away from my sister and herded away to be "scalped" by another nun, powdered with DDT (supposedly because all Indians were lice-infested) and then showered with severely hot water. Once we were stripped of all our remembrances of home, we were given the standard school-issue clothing and assigned to specific quarters.
>
> Janice Acoose

> I remember the first day at school quite vividly. My father couldn't come because he was already ill, so Mom took my brothers and I to school. I was very shy, not knowing what this was all about. I felt afraid after mom left. I was just a little guy....
>
> The first night in the dorm I felt apprehensive and cried underneath the covers as I listened to other kids crying. I knew some of the kids because a lot of them were relatives, but I didn't understand what was happening to us. All I knew was that mom and dad weren't there. I was just so damned scared.
>
> Phil Fontaine

The student teachers and I created two Roles on the Wall and recorded words to describe the feelings experienced by Janice Acoose and Phil Fontaine as children who had been forcibly separated from their families.

I asked the As to sit on one side of the room and the Bs to sit on the other side. I placed an empty suitcase in the middle of the room and I asked the As to come up one at a time, in role as a parent of one of the children, and to place an artifact into their child's suitcase. As they did so, they were to tell us why they wished this object to be part of their child's life for the next ten months. The student teachers chose items from a variety of artifacts: small packages of cookies, a knitted hat, a family photograph, a prayer, a yo-yo, a letter, a small change purse filled with coins, a Bible, a picture book, a feather, a knitted sweater, a pair of skates, a baseball hat, a scarf, a bottle of water, and so on.

One student came to the centre of the room, chose an object, placed it in the suitcase, and said:

> I place this photograph of Janice's grandmother in her suitcase so that she will remember her and that her family loves her. I pray that her grandmother's spirit looks after her and brings her back home safely.

Once the suitcase had been packed, I asked the Bs to read one of the primary source monologues I had given to them out loud to the class. Then I asked them one by one to come to the center of the room and unpack the artifact that their family member had given to them while saying a few words about the object, for example:

> Here are my new skates that my dad gave me before I left. I have no idea if we will be allowed to skate here like we did at home. I miss home so much already and I have only been here a few hours. I think I will hide the skates in case I am not allowed to have them. I wonder where I will put them?

The experience was an emotional one as my student teachers took turns both packing and unpacking the objects. In the discussion afterwards, in which we figuratively "unpacked" the experience, the students talked about how each object took on enormous meaning as they held it in their hands. One student commented, "I have been listening to the news about the apology to the First Nations peoples concerning their abusive treatment in residential schools. I did not understand the sadness and the loss until today when I was inside the experience. I know that we can never really know what it was like, but as I held my grandmother's picture I felt just incredible powerlessness."

I told my student teachers that another way that we could have done the exercise was to have each *object* speak. They were fascinated by the new knowledge that objects could not only speak but also write, and in so doing can tell hidden truths about what they have witnessed.

Many First Nations peoples speak of wanting and needing to heal. It became clear as we explored the meaning of artifacts together that all of us have to participate in some way in that healing. The Canadian government's apology is just the beginning.

The Island

The Island tells the story of a man who is washed up on the shore of a village with literally nothing on his back. He is found by the villagers, who are frightened by his strangeness and are anxious about what to do with him. They lock him up in a goat pen. He manages to escape and he pleads with the villagers to give him some food. The villagers invent all sorts of reasons why it would be detrimental to accept the newcomer into their society. Only one villager challenges the others' actions and beliefs, but he is drowned out by strident voices and punished himself. At the end of the story, the stranger is forced back onto his raft and pushed out to sea.

When I first read this story in a bookstore in England, I was reminded of two plays: *The Komagata Maru Incident* by Sharon Pollock and *A Sleep of Prisoners* by Christopher Fry.

Just as in *A Sleep of Prisoners*, the dilemmas that *The Island* presents to readers are "soul-sized," requiring us to look deep within ourselves to ask ourselves questions about who we are, what we believe in, what it means to look after each other—and what it means to do the "right thing."

The Island also reminded me of the *Komagata Maru* incident so brilliantly portrayed in Sharon Pollock's play. In May, 1914, 376 people (24 Muslims, 12 Hindus, and 340 Sikhs who were British citizens) left Hong Kong on a chartered ship called the *Komagata Maru* en route to Vancouver. The passengers, who were originally from India, hoped to settle in Canada. They were, in fact, challenging a law—passed in 1908 following anti-Asian riots in Vancouver—that required immigrants from Asia to make a continuous journey from their homeland to Canada in order to settle there. The legislation has been criticized as discriminatory because at the time there was no direct passage available from India. The passengers aboard the *Komagata Maru* were denied entry to Canada and the ship lay anchored off Vancouver for many months. Armed guards circled the ship day and night. The passengers were treated like prisoners and they were not allowed to contact their family and friends in Vancouver.

Members of the Indo-Canadian community in Vancouver pleaded with the Canadian government to allow the passengers entry to Canada, but their pleas fell on deaf ears. After two months, the passengers and crew were chased out of Vancouver by *Rainbow*, the mightiest of Canada's navy ships. When the passengers disembarked in Calcutta in September, the Viceroy of India ordered his troops to open fire on the passengers and a number of them were killed.

This event represents a dark stain on Canada's immigration history. Although the Canadian government issued an official apology to the Indo-Canadian community in 2008, that community was upset because the Prime Minister uttered the apology in a Vancouver park rather than in Parliament.

Entry Points: Responding to Images

The Island seemed to present an ideal opportunity to explore issues related to the theme of "doing the right thing." I realized that I could use this picture book in intermediate/senior classrooms to elicit conversations about our moral obligations to one another. I have worked with this book in several classrooms and I have never begun the same way. Here are three different entry points:

Entry Point 1: Comparing and Contrasting Pictures

I begin by displaying an overhead of Edvard Munsch's painting *The Scream*. I hand out index cards and I ask the students to write down the following stems on their card:

I see…

I wonder…

I imagine…

I then ask the students a few questions to help them complete their responses on the cards, for example: What do they see in this painting? What colours, lines, and shapes guide their responses to it? What do they find mysterious about the painting? What do they wonder about? What different scenarios can they imagine? How does the painting make them feel?

Students share their writing with a partner and a class discussion about their thoughts, feelings, and reactions ensues. I then show the students the illustration in *The Island* depicting what the villagers looked like when the man escaped from the cage. They again respond to this picture through writing as we compare and contrast the Edvard Munsch painting with the visual in the book.

Entry Point 2: Story/Word Punctuation

I once worked in a Grade 9 English class with *The Island*. The teacher was interested in finding ways to stimulate writing in role, so I focused on writing as I planned the unit. I began by showing the class all the illustrations in *The Island* first, without reading the text. I played music and asked the students to "take the pictures into their imaginations." I turned the pages slowly and made sure everyone could see the images. I then led a discussion about the students' initial impressions of the illustrations by asking questions such as:

- What images do you think are the most powerful?
- Which do you think is the most striking picture? Why?
- Would the pictures have been as powerful if they had been in color instead of in black and white?
- What is your overall impression of the images in the book?
- What do you predict the story is about?

I showed the students the illustrations again and asked them to write down the first words that came to mind. They wrote these words on an index card and kept it close at hand as I began reading the story.

After introducing the story, I said: "As I reread the book, I will stand by various students in the room. When I stand beside your desk, I will pause in the reading of the story. When I do, I want you to say *one* of the words that you have written on your card. In other words, the story that I am reading out loud will be 'punctuated' by your thoughts that you will express out loud. You can choose any word that you think is appropriate when I stand beside your desk." Then I began:

> Me: In the morning the people of the island found a man sitting on the shore
> Student: ALONE, DESOLATE, ISOLATED
> Me: there where fate and the ocean currents had set him and his frail raft in the night.
> Student: FEAR
> Me: When he saw them coming towards him, he rose to his feet.
> Student: COURAGE
> Me: He was not like them.
> Student: DESPAIR

Entry Point 3: Staging Tableaux

I read *The Island* to the students and ask them to form groups of four or five. I invite them to brainstorm the story before the story. Where had the man come from? How did he happen to be on the raft? What was his former life like? Then I ask the students to arrange themselves into three different tableaux that tell the man's life story. As a class, we re-create the various tableaux and begin to "paint a picture" with our bodies to represent who this man is.

Drawing and Writing

Once the students have created their tableaux and presented them to the class, I ask them to close their eyes and listen as I use a voiceover technique:

> It is the end of the third day that the man has been imprisoned in the goat pen. He has received no food from the farmer and has only been able to drink some water from a filthy bucket that he found in the corner of the pen. There is not much water left. He is growing desperate. He has no clothing and the sun bakes down all day long. He is angry, desolate, disappointed, scared, but determined to survive. He finds an old stick and begins to draw and write....

I ask the students to re-form their tableaux groups to create the writing and etchings that they imagine the man had scratched on the wall of the goat pen. Just like many prisoners, he is intent on recounting his experience and leaving his mark even if no one ever reads his story.

Before students begin to write, I pose these questions:

- What was the man trying to communicate?
- Who did he suppose would read his writing and view his etchings?
- Why was he driven to write words and make etchings on the wall?
- What might his words and images look like?

After they complete their writing, I ask the students to share their responses to the following questions with another group:

- What did the man communicate?
- How did he communicate his message?
- What did his writing look like?
- Do you think that his writing will ever be seen or deciphered by anyone?

Students then engage in a class discussion centered on these questions:

- What should the people in the village do for the man?
- Why do they behave as they do toward the man?
- What kinds of feelings and ideas are driving their actions?
- There are probably other people in the village who agree with the fisherman. They are a small group but they can make a difference. What could they do to help the stranger?
- Do you know of anyone who has experienced rejection and discrimination in the way that the stranger we read about in *The Island* did? If so, would you feel comfortable telling his or her story?
- How difficult is it to do the right thing in the face of resistance?
- What is a conscience?
- Why is it important to listen to your conscience?

You cannot make yourself feel something you do not feel, but you can make yourself do right in spite of your feelings.

Pearl S. Buck

Other Writing Activities

Here are some other writing activities that students enjoy doing after their teachers have read *The Island* to them:

Message in a Bottle: Have students write a message that the man puts in a bottle once he has been expelled from the village. What does he say about his treatment? What can he say that will stay with the villagers for the rest of their lives? What can he write that will have an impact on whoever finds the message washed up on shore?

Diary Entries: The fisherman wants to help the stranger. Have the students write his diary entries before the stranger is expelled from the village. What is he attempting to do? Why? How does he feel as he encounters resistance from others in the village? Is there anyone in his life to whom he can turn for support? What does the fisherman write in his diary after the stranger has been expelled?

Letters: The villagers have difficulty sleeping since expelling the man from the island and even when they can sleep, their dreams are haunted by what they did to the man. Although they have built a wall around the village, they cannot forget their deeds. Some of them have begun writing letters to people who live outside their village, describing their recurring nightmares.

Alternative Endings: If you were going to create another ending for this book, what would it be? How would the rest of the story unfold: after the man has been put on the raft and expelled from the village? after the fisherman's boat has been burned? after the wall has been built?

Research Similar Stories: What other stories does *The Island* remind you of? Research similar stories or historical events such as the *Komagata Maru* incident and record the ways in which the newcomers in these other stories were treated. How were their experiences similar to the stranger's? How were they different?

Angelica-Leslie

> The measure of a country's greatness should be based on how well it cares for its most vulnerable populations.
>
> Mahatma Ghandi

I was once invited to use drama in several Grade 9 Family Studies classrooms to help students understand parental responsibilities. The formal expectations in the Ontario Family Studies curriculum ask that students "analyze the impact of how changes in society affect individuals and families; understand and apply a variety of problem-solving and decision-making skills, grounded in psychological and sociological studies, to family and social problems; analyze how a changing society affects individuals and families; and describe strategies by which individuals and family members manage resources in a changing environment."

I was scheduled to meet the students in the classes on a Friday and begin the work the following week. Just a few months previously, on a bitterly cold morning in January, a baby had been discovered face-down on freezing concrete in a parking garage stairwell in Toronto about two hours after she had been abandoned. Videotaped images from a security camera showed fuzzy pictures of a figure leaving the baby, getting back into a car, and driving off. In one of the Family Studies classes, we began to talk about this news story that had riveted everyone's attention for weeks. I noticed that the students' attitudes toward the parents were judgemental and condemning. What kind of monsters would abandon a baby in the middle of a Canadian winter? "They must be cokeheads," one student remarked.

I sensed that this story could lead to all sorts of new understandings about parenthood. True wisdom involves doubting, wondering, and thinking about what you think you know, and I wanted the students to step away from their strong gut reaction to the story to investigate other possible perspectives. What had happened to the baby was wrong—I had no quarrel with that—but I wanted the students to imagine the circumstances that might have led up to such a desperate act. I am always relieved when comments during class discussions take on tentative qualities such as: "But if you think about it another way..."; "If you look at it from the mother's perspective..."; "We don't really know what was going on in that family.."; "Do we know for sure that...?"

Creating a "Protected Bower" of Analysis

I have been influenced by the work of Dorothy Heathcote, a brilliant British educator whose writing has encouraged me to think of ways to take students into a "protected bower" of analysis by changing the time, place, roles, environments, and identities featured in a story. In this way, students can become involved in the incident from various perspectives and then step back to analyze the characters, motivations, feelings, misunderstandings, contexts, and circumstances from a distance.

I went home that weekend and invented a new story. I changed the time, place, and other particulars of the incident so that the focus could shift from the real story to a similar story. I knew that we all needed to step away from the details related to the real baby and her family—especially since the case was under investigation by the Toronto police department. Therefore, I created the following brief, fictitious newspaper article. I changed the date to 30 years ago; I changed the location from a parking lot to a subway; and I made the people who discovered the abandoned baby people more or less the same age as the students with whom I would be working.

> From *The Toronto Star*, November 12, 1978
>
> A baby approximately 8 months old was found in the washroom of a subway station by a group of Grade 9 students who were on their way home from a field trip to a downtown museum. The baby was warmly wrapped and appeared to be in good health other than having a small cut above the left eye that required stitches. The students notified the subway officials, who got in touch with the local authorities. The baby has not yet been claimed.

On Monday morning I was scheduled to work with two different classes. In my introduction to the lesson, I explained that I wanted to find out whether we could use a fictional story to open our hearts and minds to the real story that had been in the news. I asked the students to form small groups of five or six. I handed out large pieces of newsprint and colored markers. I asked the groups to appoint a recorder.

I then gave one copy of the newspaper article to each group. I read the article out loud to the class. I asked them to note the date of the article—30 years ago. I then asked them to write the following question at the top of their sheet of newsprint:

What Do We Know for Sure?

The students recorded the facts of the story. We shared the facts as a class. Then I asked the students to record this question on their sheet of newsprint:

What Do We Want to Know?

I asked the students to brainstorm all the unanswered questions they had concerning the information in the brief newspaper article. Here are some of the questions they recorded:

- Was the baby a boy or a girl?
- Was the baby crying when the Grade 9 students discovered it?
- Where was the baby in the washroom? In a sink? On the floor? In a stall?
- Was the baby clean or dirty?
- Was the baby physically or mentally challenged?
- Was there anyone in the washroom when the students discovered the baby?
- How long had the baby been in the washroom?
- Why had it taken so long for the baby to be discovered?
- What did the students do immediately after they found the baby?
- What did the students do about the baby's bleeding cut?
- How many stitches did it take to close the wound?
- Was there a note left with the baby?
- Was there a diaper bag or food left with the baby?
- Was the subway official sympathetic?
- What happened after the police were called?
- How did the police react to the baby?

Questioning in Role

I asked the students to take turns playing the role of the police investigators. I said that I would play the role of one of the students who had found the baby. In role, the students were to ask me the questions they had generated in their small groups.

As the students questioned me in role as police investigators, I told them what I knew and the details related to the incident gradually became clearer. I said:

> A group of girls and boys from our class were waiting for me outside the washroom. I had gone in and then discovered the baby in one of the stalls on the floor. It had just started to cry. I looked around to see if there was anyone in the washroom but found no one there. I picked the baby up and brought it outside. We took the baby upstairs to the ticket collector. She called the police and told us to wait until they came. One of us had Kleenex—so we used that

to try to stop the bleeding. As we were waiting for the police, a large crowd gathered. They kept asking us questions. We did not know if there was a note left with the baby. There might have been one attached to the inside of the blanket but we did not discover one. The baby appeared to be normal in terms of physical and intellectual capabilities. It cried all the time that we were waiting for the police. It must have been hungry.

I stopped the role-playing and invited students' comments, some of which are reproduced here:

The baby must have just started to cry when the student discovered it. If it had been crying earlier, somebody else would have seen it.

Not necessarily. People might have seen it and just ignored it.

You can't just ignore a baby.

Sure you can. Some people just don't want to become involved in other people's issues.

Maybe the baby was drugged by the person who left it in the washroom and that was why it was so quiet. Then when the drugs wore off, it started to cry.

Maybe it had just been left there minutes before.

What I don't get is how the cut did not drain the baby of all of its blood?

It couldn't have been that big a cut.

But the wound required stitches….

Yeah. Hmmm….

The class ended. I was to come back in two days. I asked the students to reflect on the story that we had created together and to imagine who could tell us more about the incident.

Two days later, I began the class by asking the students to get into the same small groups as in the previous class. I placed an envelope on each group's table and asked the students not to touch it. Each envelope had "Secure Information: Police Services" typed in bold letters on it. There was a sense of great anticipation in the class. Finally, I asked the students to open the envelopes carefully. Inside was a note (a fictitious one I had written) that had been pinned to the inside of the baby's blanket. It said: "Take care of this little one. There was nothing more I could do."

On the chalkboard I wrote three questions: Who could have written this note? When was it written? What is the story that led to the writing of this note?

Prepared Improvisation

I asked the students to create a one-minute scene that explained why the note had been written. Students conjured various scenarios. One depicted an abusive father who could not stand the baby's crying. Another depicted a couple who could not afford their fourth child. Another shared a story of a teenage girl whose boyfriend did not like the attention that she gave the baby. We shared the scenes as a class.

I then asked the class to brainstorm all of the people or objects that could tell us the story of what had really happened to the baby (I reminded them that the baby had been abandoned 30 years ago): "If we were able to interview people or objects today that could tell us the real story, who would those people be?" The students gave me eighteen possibilities:

1. The police
2. The neighbor who lived in the apartment beside the baby's family
3. The babysitter
4. The baby
5. The baby's siblings
6. The mother
7. The father
8. The person who saw the baby being abandoned and said nothing
9. The baby's present psychiatrist
10. The baby's grandmother
11. One of the Grade 9 students who found the baby
12. The Children's Aid Worker who found an adoptive family for the baby
13. The adoptive mother
14. The blanket the baby was wrapped in at the time of the abandonment
15. The doctor who examined the baby and stitched up the baby's eye
16. The scar over the baby's eye
17. The ticket taker
18. The students' Grade 9 teacher

The students then brainstormed all the questions they still had about what had happened to this baby, and why.

Role-playing

We pushed aside the desks and the students sat in a circle on chairs. I placed five chairs in the center of the circle and asked for five volunteers. I asked these volunteers to examine the list of people we had generated and to choose one of these people to role-play. The volunteers stepped out of the classroom and shared their choices with me. One chose the role of the subway ticket-taker; another chose the role of the doctor; the other three chose the role of the neighbor, the Children's Aid worker, and the baby's biological mother. I asked the volunteers not to talk to one another but, when they re-entered the classroom, to ensure that each person's contribution to the shared storytelling would jibe with the stories of the others as they improvised them in front of the class.

We re-entered the classroom. I began: "Thirty years later—in 2008—the public still has questions about the baby that was abandoned years ago in a subway washroom. Now the public will have a chance, in a formal investigation, to learn the truth or part of the truth underlying the story of the abandoned baby." I asked the first volunteer to sit on the chair in the center of the circle. In the role of the ticket-taker, he recounted what had happened on the day of the abandonment. The class asked him questions. Then we heard from the other role-players in succession. The neighbor talked about how the girl, her boyfriend, and the baby appeared to be fine in public but at night she could hear terrible fighting through the walls.

The students asked the neighbor if she had ever phoned 911. She had not. "Why not?" asked the students. "It didn't seem worth the hassle," she answered.

"I just don't like to get involved in people's lives." "Even when a child's life is in danger?" a student countered. "Yup," replied the neighbor. The Children's Aid worker did not reveal much. She said that legal considerations prevented her from disclosing confidential information.

Finally, the girl in role as the baby's mother confessed to allowing the baby to be taken from her by her boyfriend. They had run out of money and were under a lot of stress. They fought all the time. Her boyfriend was jealous of the baby. He had been abused as a child and was becoming physically abusive toward the baby's mother. She felt it was only a matter of time before he would begin hitting the baby. She therefore allowed him to take the baby away. She felt it was the only way that the baby could remain safe. She herself had written the note. She hoped that the baby would be rescued and would find a better life.

The students posed many questions to the mother:

- Why had she remained silent all these years?
- Did she ever try to find her child?
- Would she like to meet her grown-up daughter?
- If she did, what would she say to her?
- Did she feel guilty about what she had done?
- How would she have felt if the baby had not been discovered and had died?
- Was she still involved with the baby's father?
- Did the baby's father get help to deal with his abuse issues?

The questions went on and on….

Reconnecting to the Real Story of Angelica-Leslie

During the next class, I brought in a newspaper clipping related to the real story about the baby who had been abandoned in the stairwell. "Parents of abandoned baby Angelica-Leslie arrested," the headline proclaimed. The parents, a married couple, were both 30 years old and were now living in Kitchener, west of Toronto. They had been charged with four charges under the Criminal Code: abandoning a child under the age of 10, failing to provide the necessities of life, assault causing bodily harm, and criminal negligence. I was interested in the students' reaction to this development following the work we had done together.

The class discussion that ensued took on a very different tone than it had a week earlier when we had begun our exploration of the Angelica-Leslie case. The students were now able to ask themselves: "What were the circumstances that had led these 30-year-old parents to perform such a desperate act? What was the story behind this story? How did these parents feel when they abandoned their baby? How do they feel now? What questions will the police ask them? Who was at fault? Why did the parents not come forward when the baby was discovered? What would your defense be if you were caught and charged with a similar crime? What can society do to make sure that these kinds of events don't happen again?"

The issue of blame became part of the discussion. Who is at fault when crimes such as these occur? The conversation deepened when one of the students stated simply, "Poverty and abuse are the real perpetrators of this crime." I wrote this statement on the chalkboard and the classroom teacher decided that this statement would be the springboard for the next class. She seemed delighted that the work in drama that the students had done had led them right into the meat and bones of the Family Studies curriculum.

By means of the role-playing associated with the invented story, the students were able to distance themselves from the real story. In their roles as people who had some stake in the fiction that we had created together as a class, the students could focus on the complexities of human experience and to think about the situation from many different perspectives. At the end of the workshops, they were able to talk about the real story with new eyes, ears, and hearts. Because they had been allowed to work through ideas, thoughts, assumptions, prejudices, and questions within the "protected bower" of drama, they were now more than willing to be less judgemental about the real story they were reading about in the newspapers. At the time of the printing of this book, we do not know the true story leading up to the abandonment of Angelica-Leslie. What the students and I discovered, nonetheless, was that human beings do terrible things for all manner of reasons and that blame for these actions can rest on many shoulders.

One must live in the middle of contradiction, because if all contradiction were eliminated at once life would collapse. There are simply no answers to some of the great pressing questions. You continue to live them out, making your life a worthy expression of leaning into the light.

Barry Lopez in *Arctic Dreams*

"The Man Who Finds That His Son Has Become a Thief"

When I am asked to work with students to uncover their ideas and assumptions about human differences and to help students learn the value of empathy, I turn to certain kinds of source material and engage in active work with the texts so that students can make meaning for themselves. Robert Probst encourages teachers to get inside the texts and work alongside their students. In "Dialogue with a Text" (1988), Probst explains, "If we accept the idea that literature ought to be significant, that readers have to assimilate it and work with it, that transforming it into knowledge is more significant than memorizing the definitions of technical terms, then we need to find some ways of bringing readers and text together, and of forcing upon readers the responsibility for making meaning of text."

Probst continues, "First efforts are very likely doomed to fail for obvious reasons: the students aren't used to it and don't trust it; we aren't used to it and haven't figured out all of its complications; it places tremendous responsibility on everyone involved, not the teacher alone; it requires that we deal with thirty evolving poems at a time rather than just one stable text; it requires that students accept a new and frightening notion of what knowledge is; and it demands a tolerance for ambiguity and digression. But if meaning is a human act rather than a footlocker full of dusty facts, then we must focus attention on the act of making meaning rather than simply on the accumulation of data. The learning is different because the students bring their various selves to the encounter."

I have worked for years with adolescents in examining how our choices affect other people. The following anecdote provides one example of how to explore this theme with students.

Teacher in Role

I was invited to work with some secondary school English students in a detention centre over three consecutive mornings. The group was a little surprised when I told them that all they had to do was sit at their desks and use their imaginations as they listened to someone speaking to them for a few minutes. I told them that when I sat on the chair in front of the teacher's desk, I was going to be somebody else—someone who was going to tell them a story. "It would help," I advised, "if you imagine that you are listening to my story in a coffee shop and that you are a friend or acquaintance of this person." I told them that I did not expect them to say anything until I "went out of role."

I had written the script below on an index card because I wanted the information to be as detailed as possible. I glanced at the card occasionally as I spoke to the students. I took my time to tell them my story in role, as though I were speaking to some friends in a coffee shop:

> Something happened today that I haven't even told his mother about. I'm still in shock, actually. That Kevin would do such a thing again is totally unbelievable. I mean after all that we have done for him—bailing him out of the last fiasco—the stolen car. You remember? I had just got in from work and the phone rang. It was the police. They told me that Kevin had been caught stealing a TV from a store. At first I told the police that it couldn't be him. Not our Kevin. He was over with all that stuff now. When the police put him on the phone, he told me that he hadn't stolen anything. "Honest," he said. The police told me to come to the store at the corner of our street. When I got there, Kevin was in the back of the police car at the front of the building. They wouldn't let me see him at first and waved me away. I went into the store and spoke to the owner. I denied that this could be true. Then a police officer came into the store and showed me the evidence on the video camera. Kevin stole the TV in broad daylight. How stupid is that? *(Pause)* Anyway, because Kevin is already "known to the police" he had to be taken down to the station. The police asked me if I wanted to come in the cruiser or follow on my own. I went home to get my car—Lily wasn't home from work yet, thank goodness. I left her a note. She will be so disappointed in Kevin—all over again. What did we do to deserve a son like this?

Asking Questions Out of Role

After I had spoken, I stood up from the chair to indicate that I was "out of role." I asked the class to answer the following questions orally:

- Who was the person who was speaking to you?
- What has happened?
- How old do you think Kevin is? Why?
- What might Kevin's police records say?
- What do you think will happen to Kevin?

Reading for Clarification

I asked the students to get into groups of five or six and I gave each group a copy of Kevin's father's monologue. They appointed one person in the group to read the monologue again. They discussed the inferences they had made about the father and his son.

Tableaux

I asked the students to create three tableaux representing the crime:

1. Kevin entering the store (Was he alone? Did he have a partner to distract the shop owner?)
2. The theft of the TV (How far did he get with the TV before he was caught?
3. Kevin being caught (Who caught him? Where?)

Each group shared their tableaux with the rest of the class.

Parallel Universes

Next, I asked the students to think about the kind of family that Kevin came from. Did he have brothers and sisters? Did he have grandparents? We created a small family tree on the chalkboard. I asked the students to think about what the mother, the father, siblings, and grandparents were doing at the exact time that Kevin had stolen the TV. Was the father driving home from work? Was the mother picking up a few groceries after work before she got on the bus to go home? Was the grandmother pouring herself a cup of tea in her small apartment? What did their lives look like? I asked small groups of students to improvise scenes showing the members of Kevin's family going about their everyday lives at the same time this boy was ruining his.

A few groups volunteered to share their parallel universes: one group showed Kevin stealing the TV and then juxtaposed this scene with an image of his mother, Lily, buying take-out as a surprise dinner for her family. Another group showed Kevin being arrested and then showed an image of Kevin's sister getting her exam marks back and receiving the highest marks in her class.

Writing in Role

I asked the students to write the note that Kevin's father had left on the kitchen table. I asked them to think of this family's history—all of the disappointments that they have experienced. How careful would Kevin's father be in writing the note to his wife so as not to alarm her? Here are two samples of the students' writing:

> Lily—
> Will be back a little late for dinner. Something's come up with Kevin— nothing serious, I don't think. Why don't you eat and I will see you later?
> Richard

> Hi
> You might be surprised that I'm not home. Don't be. Kevin and I have been delayed. Try calling my cell when you get this. Nothing to worry about….
> Love you,
> Richard

Reading and Understanding the Poem

We then read a poem by Canadian poet Raymond Souster that the students located in their poetry anthologies. The poem is titled "The Man Who Discovers

That His Son Has Become a Thief." It takes time to read and understand a poem. Students need to learn that the meaning of a poem reveals itself little by little and that readers interpret a poem in different ways during and after subsequent rereadings—and that this is part of the process of reading and understanding poetry.

I asked the students to stand in a circle. Then I had them do the following:

- read the poem silently
- read the poem one line at a time
- read the poem as if there were a question mark at the end of each line
- read the poem in light of different contexts and with different attitudes and emotions (possible contexts: in a waiting room at a jail; in a courtroom; on an airplane) (attitudes: sarcastic; pleading; detached; shell-shocked; blasé; resigned) (emotions: furious; heartbroken; listless; despondent)

Partner Work

As a next step in the lesson, I had the students read the poem with a partner. I asked them to decide who was A and who was B. The students stood back-to-back and read the poem silently. Then they faced each other and read the poem together out loud.

Next, they read every other line. Then they went back to the beginning and read every line that had been left out. For the final reading, we tried moving around the room in the following manner:

A said a line and moved to another part of the room. B followed A and spoke his/her line.

B spoke another line and changed position but remained in the same spot. A found a way of adjusting his/her stance to match/support/complement B's position.

Sequencing Emotions

I asked the students to work with a partner and to write in sequence all of the emotions that the father would have experienced as he gradually discovered that his son had become a thief. Below are some of the words that we generated. We left them on the chalkboard as we continued to explore the poem together.

Angry
Loyal
Calm
Hurt
Ashamed
Sick
Alone
Fearful
Paranoid

Improvised Telephone Conversations

I asked each student to find a partner. One student was to play Richard, the father. The other was to play, Lily, the mother. Lily calls her husband when she gets home from work and sees the note on the kitchen table. The improvisation begins with Lily's line: *Richard? Where are you? Has anything happened?* Volunteers shared their improvised telephone conversations.

Forum Theatre

As I continued the lesson, I asked for two volunteers to role-play Kevin's parents. The other students asked the volunteers a series of spontaneous questions that included:

- Why do you think your son stole the TV?
- Has Kevin always been a difficult child?
- When did you first realize that you had a problem child on your hands?
- Have you ever considered taking Kevin to a doctor?
- How have the crimes that Kevin has committed affected your lives and the lives of your family members?
- What do you hope will happen to Kevin?
- Do you have issues with your other children?

Class Discussion

The work that these students did was amazing. The most important conversations took place at the end of the classes, when the students felt sufficiently trusting and comfortable to talk about the choices they had made that had drastically altered their lives as well as the lives of their family members.

The teacher managed these conversations brilliantly, helping the students to progress from regret to dreams of what they would do differently in the future. I was deeply moved by how skillfully she instilled hope in her students. I am confident those students have gone on to lead better lives because of the encounter with a teacher who listened to them, honored them, and made them understand that there can be fresh new beginnings for everyone.

"Letter"

In my teaching, I am interested in examining and interrupting the dominant class-based power dynamics that are pervasive in our culture. As a teacher, I meet students from a wide variety of social positions and locations. I have taught in inner-city schools in which there is a diverse mix of students and in schools where most of the students come from upper-middle-class backgrounds. And I often encounter challenges—particularly when I try to help students think critically about social class and its hidden codes and rules.

I was once asked to do a series of workshops with a group of amazing elementary and secondary school teachers on the theme of anti-bullying. Toward the end of the workshops, one elementary teacher told a story about a recent bullying incident. One of her students had found twenty dollars in the playground and had handed it in at the office. His friends could not believe his "stupidity" and they railed against him for days because he had not kept the money. No amount of praise for the boys' actions from teachers could dispel the bullying that the boy had to endure. I joined the teachers in brainstorming ways that students could come to understand this boy's actions in a different light and to admire him, not torment him, for what he had done.

As we worked together, I was reminded of a short essay titled "Letter," written by Judith Mackenzie, that I enjoyed reading to high school students. When I taught in a school attended by mostly middle-class students, I introduced this essay to attempt to move them to a new understanding of what it must be like for people to live without the basic necessities of life.

I read the following text to the students:

Letter

by Judith Mackenzie

When I was eight years old, my father, a union organizer, in the forties and fifties was blacklisted, accused of communist activities. It meant no work—with a vengeance. My mother, then in her forties, had twin boys that spring—premature, and in premedicare times you can imagine the devastating costs for their care. I was hungry that year, hungry when I got up, hungry when I went to school, hungry when I went to sleep. In November, I was asked to leave school because I only had boys' clothes to wear—hand-me-downs from a neighbor. I could come back, they said, when I could dress like a lady.

The week before Christmas, the power and the gas were disconnected. We ate soup made from carrots, potatoes, cabbage and grain meant to feed chickens, cooked on our wood garbage burner. Even as an eight-year old, I knew the kind of hunger we had was nothing compared to people in India and Africa. I don't think we could have died in our middle-class Vancouver suburb. But I do know that the pain of hunger is intensified and brutal when you live in the midst of plenty. As Christmas preparations increased, I felt more and more isolated, excluded, set apart. I felt a deep abiding hunger for more than food. Christmas Eve day came, grey and full of the bleak, sleety rain of a west-coast winter. Two women, strangers, struggled up our driveway, loaded down with bags. They left before my mother answered the door. The porch was full of groceries—milk, butter, bread, cheese and Christmas oranges. We never knew who they were, and after that day, pride being what it was, we never spoke of them again. But I am forty-five years old, and I remember them well.

Since then I've crafted a life of joy and independence, if not of financial security. Several years ago, living in Victoria, my son and I were walking up the street, once more in west-coast sleet and rain. It was just before Christmas and we were, as usual, counting our pennies to see if we had enough for all our festive treats, juggling these against the necessities. A young man stepped in front of me, very pale and carrying an old sleeping bag, and asked for spare change—not unusual in downtown Victoria. No, I said, and walked on. Something hit me like a physical blow about a block later. I left my son and walked back to find the young man. I gave him some of our Christmas luxury money—folded into a small square and tucked into his hand. It wasn't much, only ten dollars, but as I turned away, I saw the look of hopelessness turn into amazement and then joy. Well, said the rational part of my mind. Judith, you are a fool, you know he's just going up the street to the King's Hotel and spend it on drink or drugs. You've taken what belongs to your family and spent it on a frivolous romantic impulse. As I was lecturing myself on gullibility and sensible charity, I noticed the young man with the sleeping bag walking quickly up the opposite side of the street, heading straight for the King's. Well, let this be a lesson, said the rational Judith. To really rub it in, I decided to follow him. Just before the King's, he turned into a corner grocery store. I watched through the window, through the poinsettias and the stand-up Santas. I watched him buy milk, butter, bread, cheese and Christmas oranges.

Now, I have no idea how that young man arrived on the street in Victoria, nor will I ever have any real grasp of the events that had led my family to a dark and hungry December. But I do know that charity cannot be treated as an RRSP. There is no best investment way to give, no way to ensure value for our dollar. Like the Magi, these three, the two older women struggling up the driveway and the young man with the sleeping bag, gave me, and continue to give me, wonderful gifts—the reminder that love and charity come most truly and abundantly from an open and unjudgemental heart.

After I had finished reading, I asked the students to retell the story in small groups. Then I asked the students to find a partner. One of them played the role of the young man. The other played the role of a social worker who had experience working with panhandlers. The social worker's job was to find out the panhandler's story.

I took the panhandlers aside and told them that they should tell their story only if they felt that they could trust the social worker.

I took the social workers aside and told them that they needed to apply all their skills as social workers to find out the man's story. They needed to make the man feel respected, ask him questions without appearing to probe, and find a way to establish trust in the relationship.

The role-playing lasted about 10 minutes. Then I passed out a card and had each student write in role. I asked the social workers to write a report based on their first impressions of the homeless man. I asked the homeless man to write a letter or diary account. I then scaffolded the reading of their writing in an inner/outer circle formation, described below.

Inner/Outer Circle

The inner/outer circle strategy allowed me to orchestrate the reading of the students' writing and to enhance the reading so that everyone's voice is amplified. The group of students in the inner circle sat on chairs while the group of students in the outer circle stood. As I touched the students gently on the shoulder to cue them to read their writing, we heard different voices and different genres interplay with one another and the effect was astounding. Because I could stop the reading at any point and return to the various readers to ask them to repeat their lines, I could manipulate the overall effect of the oral reading. Weaker writers and stronger writers had opportunities to play off one another.

Lost Key Stories

I asked the students to get into groups of five and I gave one member in the group a key. I told them that this was a key to someone's home. I asked them to tell stories of losing keys. What kinds of keys did they lose? What predicaments did they find themselves in when they lost a key? Did they ever find the key? Have they ever been locked out of their home? If so, what happened? How did it feel to be locked out? The students shared their lost key stories. I wrote the following quote on the board:

"Home is where the heart is."

Then I read them an expanded quote:

"Home is where the heart is. If I have a room, is that a home? If I am not allowed cooking, hot and cold running water—is that a room or a home? I believe that it is still a room. When I am in jail I am in a room, when I am in a hospital I am in a room, but it's not a home. A room is still not a home."

I asked the students:

- Who do you think is speaking?
- Where could this person be saying these lines? In what context? At a symposium on homelessness? In a courtroom? At a police station?
- What series of incidents had made the person come to the realization that a room is not a home?
- Why is it important for this person to let other people know that a room is not a home?
- Do you think the listeners care? Are they sympathetic or judgemental? Why do you think so?

Documentary Scene

I asked the students to create a scene in which the person is saying the words in the quote. Then I asked them to create a series of tableaux depicting the incidents in the person's life that had led him or her to the point where he or she was uttering the quote. The students created a scene in which a homeless person—a woman—is picked up by the police. The quote was spoken at a police station and the homeless person's story was depicted through tableaux as she spoke.

We examined what had been created in the tableaux and talked about the homeless person's frustration and anger. The students admitted to being afraid of homeless people and not knowing what to do when they came into the local burger restaurant asking for money. "It gets really ugly," said one girl, describing the derision that the homeless person faced from the students who had plenty of money to buy their school lunches and treats.

Is There Such a Thing as a Second Chance?

How important is $10 or $20? What difference did Judith Mackenzie's gift make in the life of the young homeless man? Do small gestures count? Is there such a thing as a second chance?

As a homework assignment, I asked the students to visit Toronto's Centre for Addiction and Mental Health (CAMH) website to listen to or read the story of Frank O'Dea—once a young homeless man who received ten cents from a stranger. He made a phone call to CAMH, which changed his life. He went on to co-found the popular and very successful coffee chain called The Second Cup. In 2005, Frank O'Dea was awarded the Order of Canada. His story is powerful and transformational. Ten cents, a quarter, ten bucks, twenty dollars—*can* make a difference.

The Elephant Man

Maxine Greene, a renowned American professor of philosophy and of education, tells us that aesthetic encounters with works of art are "situated encounters." What she means by this is that all of us who look at paintings in galleries or in books, listen to music at concerts or on our ipods, witness dance or theatre performances either live, on TV, or on the Internet apprehend that piece of art in the light of our own backgrounds, biographies, and experiences. We literally bring ourselves—our identities, memories, personalities, and understandings about human relationships and the world that we inhabit—to our encounters with art. Our own varied life experiences inform how we react to the piece of art in front of us and these experiences shape highly diverse responses to what we see, hear, feel, and comprehend.

What is the role of critical pedagogy in helping students understand a piece of theatre? As teachers, we need to help students relate the characters' experiences and struggles to their own lives and to the lives of others. Finding the entry points is critical and planning what you are going to teach both before and after the play is essential. What follows is an example of entry points and lesson planning related to work with one particular play.

I was invited to work in an inner-city high school with students who were enrolled in Grade 10 Dramatic Arts and Grade 12 English classes. With my help, the teachers had organized a field trip to see *The Elephant Man* in a downtown Toronto theatre. I prepared a number of pre-performance activities to conduct with the students, some of which are outlined below.

Circular Drama

I prepared laminated cards outlining a brief description of the life of Joseph (John) Merrick, the "Elephant Man." We read the cards using an overhead projector. I then divided the class into groups and asked them to prepare a series of tableaux and small scenes to dramatize the key events in Merrick's life.

GROUP ONE
1. Joseph Carey Merrick (who later changed his name to John Merrick) was born in Leicester, England, on August 5, 1862.
2. He was a normal, healthy baby and had a younger brother and sister.
3. His deformity began developing at the age of three with small bumps appearing on the left side of his body. He was described as a wonderfully imaginative and intelligent boy.
4. His mother died when he was 12. According to family accounts, she too was "crippled."

I need theatre in all its forms and guises and formats to enter my world more fully, to help me see more clearly, to feel and think at once. I want to behold the world somehow differently. I want to be educated by theatre.

David Booth

GROUP TWO
1. Merrick's father remarried, but his stepmother did not like Joseph.
2. She sent him out to work selling shoe polish on the street.
3. As he worked, he was constantly harassed and bullied by local children.
4. His stepmother was very cruel and was always disappointed when he did not bring home enough money.

GROUP THREE
1. Merrick left home.
2. When he was 22, he took a job as a sideshow attraction and managed to earn just enough money to live.
3. A turning point in his life occurred when he was exhibited in the back of an empty shop on Mile End Road in London, where he was seen by the physician Frederick Treves.
4. Treves gave Merrick one of his cards in the event that Merrick would be willing to submit to a medical examination.

GROUP 4
1. When sideshows were outlawed in the United Kingdom in 1886, Merrick traveled to Belgium to find work.
2. There, he was mistreated.
3. Ultimately, he was abandoned by a showman, who stole Merrick's savings of 50 pounds.
4. He managed to cross the English Channel back to England.

GROUP 5
1. Merrick returned to London and inadvertently became the cause of a disturbance in the Liverpool Street train station.
2. Suffering from a severe bronchial infection and hampered by his deformities, Merrick was barely able to speak correctly.
3. However, he had taken care to retain the business card of Frederick Treves, who was called to the scene by the police.
4. In his role as physician at London Hospital, Treves arranged for Merrick to make the hospital his home.

Voices in the Head

I assigned each group of students a different card, which represented one aspect of the story in a tableau. Then I told them that when I stood beside their character they were to improvise lines that those characters might be thinking. The rest of the people in the tableau needed to remain frozen; only the character whom I was standing beside was to say the "voices in his or her head."

Split-second Scenes

Next, I asked students to create a line for each character in the tableau and I invited them to animate the image so that everyone could say their line. They were to make a split-second scene come alive.

Prepared Scenes

The students were then asked to create a more detailed scene that would give us more insight into the human side of the story, such as the scene at Merrick's mother's deathbed—her parting words to the son that she loved so much.

As the students created small scenes for each segment, a student who had been away for a while and was late appeared in the class. He needed a part in the proceedings but everyone was pretty well rehearsed at this point so I asked him to play the role of Merrick. He stood in the center of the classroom and pointed to each group and they brought their scene to life. When all the transitions had been devised, we rehearsed the new play, which the class performed for another high school class that would also attend the stage production in Toronto.

This Is Your Line

In preparation for the final assignment, I had typed lines from the play and had put them in individual envelopes with the name of each student on the outside of the envelope. A week before we attended the play, I instructed the students to open their envelope and read the line that I had given them. I asked several students to read their lines to the class. Then I told them that the line that I had given them would be *their* line. They should wait to hear it spoken as they listened to the play. Afterwards, they were to write a short paragraph on the significance of that line to them and its contribution to the meaning and overall effect of the play. Some of the lines I had extracted from the play included:

> Treves: I am a doctor. What would you have me do?
>
> Sandwich: Appearances do not daunt me.
>
> Merrick: I have a home. This is my home. This is my home. I have a home. As long as I like?
>
> Mrs. Kendal: Mr. Merrick, I must go now. I should like to return if I may. And so that we may without delay, teach you about society.

Here is a student's response to Sandwich's line:

> When I opened the envelope I had no idea who Sandwich and I can't stand not knowing things so I went to the public library and got *The Elephant Man* by Bernard Pomerance out. I read the play and it was hard for me to understand—but I did find the line. It seemed to me that Sandwich did not know herself very well. She said that appearances did not bother her but when she laid eyes on Merrick all that changed. She ran out of the room.
>
> When we went to the play, I could not believe how amazing the actor playing Merrick was. It was just amazing to watch him. He was not repulsive and yet he was; you could see why people were afraid of him and you could not understand it all at the same time. When Sandwich said "My Line"—I almost cried out loud because I knew what she was going to do at the end of the scene—run away! But it was her explanation at the end of the scene that made me sympathetic to her. Words did not prepare her for the horror of what she saw. Words were not enough and she could not handle the reality of Merrick's deformity.
>
> None of my friends had read the play before they went to the theatre. They really concentrated on listening so that they could hear their lines said out loud. I thought that this was an amazing activity because in the class discussion everyone was really involved in talking about what it was like for them when their line was said.

The Elephant Man provides us with models of language to read out loud, with complex issues to analyze, with characters' motives to interpret, with unfair circumstances and brutality to face, with metaphoric language to play with, and with a sophisticated interweaving of the play's time and place to understand.

When I was preparing activities for the classes, I asked myself: "What could the students look for?" I wanted them to feel confident when they recognized certain realities that they had learned about ahead of time. Therefore, I had them re-create Merrick's life. I knew that they would be surprised and delighted by the knowledge that they brought to the experience and that they would enjoy the play that much more.

The students thoroughly enjoyed the performance and were awestruck at how talented Brent Carver was in the role of Merrick. They were extremely impressed by the entire production. They had listened intently during the play and were deeply moved by Carver's portrayal of a man who repels people because of his physical deformity. Each student talked about what it was like to hear their line come alive and what they were thinking and wondering about when the line was spoken. Because of their encounter with this powerful play, students were humbled by what they did not understand but were also swept up in a story that gripped them from beginning to end.

"Wedding Album"

My secondary school colleagues and I talk a lot about the tensions that surface in classrooms when the topic of sexual orientation comes to the fore. One of my best friends, an inner city secondary school teacher, has almost given up trying to address this topic. She says that she feels overwhelmed by the violent homophobic statements uttered in her classrooms. She says, "I just get worried about keeping everyone—especially the gay kids—safe." She is not alone. "The pervasiveness of heterosexism has resulted in the near absence of any substantive discussions about the denial of basic civil rights to gays and lesbians in school," comments Sharon Grady in *Drama and Diversity* (p. 104).

The Toronto District School Board has developed an excellent curriculum document called *Rainbows and Triangles* (2002). This document provides helpful advice to teachers involved in anti-homophobia education. Teaching and learning about homophobia are complex processes. The document suggests that teachers and students develop a shared language and work within these definitions; deal with homophobic incidents as they arise and turn them into teachable moments; give students time to reflect on their own ideas and values; and empower students to behave in ways that challenge homophobia and heterosexism.

The document states clearly that "teachers need to spend longer than one lesson on anti-homophobia with their students." Recently, I developed a series of lessons that might help young people examine, with insight and sensitivity, the impact of homophobia on their lives, the lives of others, and society at large. I had a chance to work with material I had written for a book called *Family Ties* (Nelson, 2006). I worked for three sessions in a Grade 12 class at the end of the academic year in June. The source I used was called "Wedding Album"—a story in three emails—that I had based on a true story involving a friend of mine. I had changed the names and the location but the story resonated with me and with the students with whom I worked. The three emails tell a story of a wedding that had a positive impact on a family. The brother of the bride, the bride, and the bride's best friend send each other messages describing their thoughts and feelings about the wedding and the discussions that took place both before and after the event. The reader must read between the lines of each email to figure out the relationships and to discover the nature of the issue confronting the guests and the family both before and after the wedding.

Many of the classmates of the Grade 12 students with whom I was working were away at a music camp, so the group consisted of only 15 students. On the first day of the sessions, I asked the students to get into small groups and to talk about a family event that they had attended as a guest. The event could have taken place in their own family or in a friend's family. I asked them: "How were you welcomed into the family? Did everyone seem to be getting along or were there tensions between people as they interacted? How did you know that these tensions existed? How did you manage to read body language and make inferences in order to understand what was going on?"

There were lots of laughter and joking as students told their stories of family gatherings. I realized that these students knew each other quite well. It was the end of the year—and they had established some great friendships.

Working with Magazine Images

After the students had shared their stories, they went back to their desks. I distributed different kinds of family-oriented consumer magazines, making sure that there was one per student.

I asked each student to find three family pictures in the ads or in the articles and to cut them out and lay them on their desks. I asked them to "tag" each of the family members by giving each person a name and a relationship. Students wrote these tags right on the ads. Then I had each person share their tagged family picture with a partner. They recorded the similarities and differences on a sheet of paper in chart form (this chart is reproduced as a blackline master at the back of this book):

	Student 1	Student 2
Number of people in the family		
What are the relationships amongst the family members?		
What does the family look like in terms of race?		
What does the family look like in terms of social class? How did you infer this?		
What product is being sold in the ad?		

As we shared our findings as a class, the students were amazed to discover that 90 percent of the families in the ads they had chosen were white. All appeared to be middle class and 50 percent of the families had a well-fed dog in the picture! We talked about how these pictures were placed into mainstream media and how these magazines were geared to middle- and upper-class families. I asked the students to work with their partner to try to find pictures that represented something different from the traditional, white, middle-class family. There were no such images to be found.

Rearranging the Pictures

I asked the students to get into groups of four and to bring their ad with them. I asked them to cut out the figures in the ads and to work collectively. I asked them to rearrange the individual figures on small-sized poster paper to make a different kind of family structure. As they worked, they began to see more variety: biracial couples; two white fathers with Asian children; two-mother/single child families; two-father families; couples without children; and so on. I then asked the students why these kinds of images of families aren't found in the mainstream media. Here are some of the students' responses:

> People will not buy magazines that depict something that makes them feel uncomfortable—so the magazine publishers play it safe.

> Some people think that gay, lesbian, and bisexual people are a bad influence on children—so they are careful how they portray families.

> I buy lots of magazines that show different kinds of relationships. I would never even look at these kinds of magazines because they don't speak to me.

I began the next class by distributing the first email from "Wedding Album" to each group of four students:

To: snugger@email.ca
From: gtl@email.ca

Hi Lucy:

Just wanted to thank you so much for inviting Steve and me to the wedding. You looked even more beautiful than I could have imagined and I was so happy that I was your big brother watching my kid sister going down that aisle! Everything was perfect, wasn't it? Dad and Mom got along even though it was slightly awkward. It was good to see Dad after all these years. We even talked a bit. The weather finally cooperated. The tent did not blow away and the dance was awesome. Steve and I had a great time. My feet are still sore from all that dancing.

Call us when you get back from the honeymoon and we'll come over to admire all of your wedding presents.

Love,

Greg

I handed out chart paper to each of the groups. I asked them to write at the top of the chart:

Information That We Know for Sure

The students worked for ten minutes. I instructed them to not make any inferences but to just write down the facts. We pooled our fact sheets and came up with the following list:

> Lisa is Greg's sister.
> Greg has emailed Lisa.
> Lisa has just been married and is on her honeymoon.
> Greg and Steve came to the wedding.
> Greg danced at the wedding.
> Greg and Lisa's father and mother were at the wedding. They got along although it was awkward.
> Greg and his father talked "a bit" at the wedding.
> The wedding was conducted in fine weather.
> Steve and Greg had a good time.

I then distributed the second email to the group:

To: mkl@email.com
From: snugger@email.ca

Hi Mom:

Thanks for your phone message. We got to Quebec City safely even though we were really tired after the wedding. We talked all the way there and analyzed every moment of our wedding day. Thanks for all that you did to make everything so perfect—including the cake. I think everybody enjoyed themselves. Steve and Greg seemed to have a great time and I don't think anyone made any stupid comments to them or behind their backs so your worries about the guests being cruel were groundless. It was really important that they were both there and I am glad that I stood up to Dad and insisted that Steve accompany Greg. I actually noticed the three of them talking at some point before the dance started so I breathed a sigh of relief. Maybe Dad is realizing how much he loves Greg and how stupid he has been about Steve. It is time to enter the 21st century!!!!

Will call you when we get more settled. Thanks again for being such a great MOM.

Love,

Lucy

Once again, I asked students to record just the facts on the sheets of paper. Afterwards, we shared the facts as a whole class (see the following page).

Lisa and her new husband went to Quebec City for their honeymoon.

They arrived safely.

They analyzed the wedding on their way there.

Lisa had insisted that Steve accompany her brother Greg to the wedding.

She had stood up to her father.

Steve and Lisa's father talked at the wedding.

Lisa does not think that any guests made stupid comments about Steve and Greg.

Lisa's mother had something to do with the wedding cake.

Finally, I distributed the third email to each group and had them repeat the activity.

To; snugger@email.ca
From: laila@email.ca

Dear Lucy:

I loved being your Maid of Honor!!!! It was an awesome experience although I can't believe how much I laughed and then cried and then laughed some more. Everybody thought you looked amazingly beautiful. Glad that you decided not to wear that freaky veil. You looked better with just that beautiful flower in your hair.

The dance was a big hit. Everyone had a ball.

Just had to tell you what happened yesterday. I went to get a snack before class and I met your Dad and a number of the guys who were at the wedding lining up to get a coffee. They were all chatting and laughing and then somebody made a snide comment about Steve and Greg dancing. There was an awkward silence because they saw that I was in line too. But you know what your Dad said? He said, "I saw nothing unusual at the wedding. I just saw a lot of young people having a great time and that included my son and his friend Steve. Now, if you will excuse me, I need to get back to work."

I wanted to run after him and hug him because I saw that he had a tear in his eye. But I didn't. I really wanted you to hear that story. It made me feel so good for your family.

I love weddings!!!

Call me when you get back from you honeymoon.

Love,

Laila

Here was the class's collective response:

Laila was Lucy's maid of honor.

She had a good time at the wedding.

Laila is a student and is still in school.

At a coffee shop, she overheard a conversation between someone who made a cruel comment about Steve and Greg.

Greg and Lisa's father was in the line-up and heard the comment too.
She witnessed Lisa's father's response.
Lisa's father defended Greg and Steve.
He teared up as he spoke in their defense.
Lisa is still on her honeymoon.

Forum Theatre

I then asked the students to talk about what was really going on in terms of the family dynamic before, during, and after the wedding and to create a scene that depicted one of the following:

- Lisa's determination to convince her father that Steve must accompany Greg to the wedding.
- The scene between Greg and his father at the wedding.
- The scene between Greg, Steve, and the father at the wedding.
- The scene in the coffee shop.

Each group prepared the scene. I then introduced the class to the idea of Forum Theatre. In Forum Theatre, a small group of "performers" acts out their scene for the rest of the class, who are the "observers." Both the performers and the observers have the right to stop the drama at any point and make suggestions as to how it might proceed. For instance, an observer might stop the drama and ask for it to be replayed with changes designed to bring out another point of view or focus. I made it clear to the class that all of us—performers as well as observers—had to take responsibility for the crafting of the scene and that we would be using the Forum Theatre technique to uncover the subtext of the story that we were creating. Uncovering the subtext would help us find out how this family and the guests at the wedding had responded to the presence of Greg and Steve at Lisa's wedding.

We began with the scene between Greg and his father at the wedding. The performers explained that the scene was very short—the father and son were interrupted by the beginning of the speeches at the wedding banquet. We watched the scene and witnessed the awkward beginnings of a conversation between a son and his father. The observers then changed the scene in the following ways: "Let's try it with no interruptions; let's try it with Greg confronting his father for his lack of communication; let's do the scene again and this time, even though they want to talk to each other, no one is willing to say the first word."

Each time the performers and the observers reworked the scene, the pain in the father-son relationship, Greg's hurt feelings, and the ramifications of the father's homophobic feelings toward his son's relationship, were moving and troubling. The scenes opened up candid conversations about the students' own assumptions and feelings about homophobia.

Hot Seating

On the third and final day, I decided to play the part of the father so that the students could question me about my motives, values, relationships, and actions. The students worked in groups to prepare their questions. I set up a scenario for them. "It has been three months since Lisa's wedding and Greg's father has become more and more accepting of his son and his friend Steve." I told them,

"You are all reporters doing a story about family relationships and you have an opportunity to interview Greg's father. He is getting on in years—so you need to be respectful."

In role as Greg's father, I answered the questions posed by the journalists. I talked about my regret over the lost years with my son and about how I had grown in my understanding of all the different kinds of relationships that can exist in the world.

I then asked for volunteers to role-play other family members. One girl played Lisa's and Greg's mother. A boy who played Steve told his story carefully, describing feelings of sadness and rejection.

Writing in Role

The journalists then chose one of these people and wrote an email to thank them for granting them interviews. Here is one example:

To: Steve@email.com
From: Tara @news_of_the_nation.com

Thank you very much for meeting with me yesterday to help me write a news-paper story about contemporary family life. Your story about being excluded from your partner's family because of your sexual orientation touched me deeply. I really appreciated your willingness to talk.

I think that it is pretty amazing that you are able to forgive Greg's father for what he said about you in the past. You told us that he ignored you for over five years and did not talk to his son during that time—not even when Greg's grandmother died. I could not believe that! I am surprised that Greg finds that he is able to forgive and forget. He was apparently really close to his grandma.

I am still not sure what it was that brought the father around—you weren't very clear about that. Did the emotion of his daughter's wedding affect him in some strange way? You hinted that the father might be unwell. Maybe that was why he suddenly agreed to speak to his son and even defend him in public.

Anyway, thank you for agreeing to talk to all the press.

We will be running the story in a couple of weeks and I will be sure to send you your own copy.

Yours sincerely,

Tara

Can homophobia be extinguished in our classrooms? This work is enormously difficult and can cause eruptions of language that are offensive and shameful. Therefore, clear rules of engagement in the classroom must be set and adhered to: Do not speak words that are hurtful. My hope is that if students cannot speak the words, then the time spent thinking them will be diminished as well.

In a book titled *Moral Grandeur and Spiritual Audacity*, Susannah Heschel refers to her famous father, an American rabbi and one of the leading Jewish theologians of the 20th century who marched in the Selma Civil Rights March with Martin Luther King, Jr. in 1965. Heschel comments on the importance that her father placed on words: "He used to remind us that the Holocaust did not begin with the building of crematoria, and Hitler did not come to power with tanks and guns; it all began with the uttering of evil words, with defamation, with language and propaganda. Words create worlds, he used to tell me when I was a child. They must be used very carefully. Some words, once having been uttered, gain eternity and can never be withdrawn."

The Diary of Anne Frank

Contemporary research examining memory and memorial underscores the fact that in provoking history as an act of remembrance for a new generation, we are narrating a sense of self. The paradox of retelling these personal and public histories is that we are playing out that which cannot be represented.

Belarie Zatzman

Bleema Getz, a former student and now a close friend of mine, taught for many years in a downtown Toronto high school. She taught English and Dramatic Arts and has been a model for young teachers eager to learn about drama in education. The following is a description of an encounter between her immigrant students and the play, *The Diary of Anne Frank*.

The year had been a difficult one. I had finished my treatments for breast cancer and was returning to work as a drama teacher who teaches in an inner-city high school. This was to be my 30th year teaching and would turn out to be the most significant.

I entered my senior drama class and was delighted and relieved to find 10 students—a drama teacher's dream, especially mine because I wanted to direct a play with my graduating class and often found the numbers too high. After our initial "hellos" and "how was your summer?" my students let me know that I had been missed and that they were so happy to have me back. These kids, these wonderful kids made me feel like family. And then came the big question. "So, what play will we be producing this year?" I didn't know. I had been waiting to find out the numbers and who was in the class. "I'll let you know in time."

By the time the winter break arrived, I knew the play we would be working on and I knew who would be cast in each role. I had wanted to produce *The Diary of Anne Frank* for a long time. Now I knew I had the cast to do so.

January 3, the class entered the drama room eager to finally find out my choice of play, eager to find out their part, eager to begin, eager to learn their lines. But they would have to wait for a week.

I had planned a series of workshops to help them understand the journey that they were about to embark on. Little did I know that the play would not be the major drama.

Workshop #1: "Find a place in the room so you can be alone and sit or lie down and get comfortable. You will be there for the duration of the period—70 minutes. You cannot get up or talk. You must be very quiet. You can read or nap but you must be completely solitary and silent."

When the bell rang to end the class, I told the students that I would see them the next day. Some students looked blurry-eyed, others confused. They left quietly with great curiosity.

Workshop #2: When they arrived the next day, a pile of clothes in the middle of the room greeted them: winter coats, scarves, shirts, skirts, and pants. "Put on as many clothes as you can but try to look somewhat normal. When ready, walk around the school for 20 minutes and then return."

As they took off the extra clothes upon their return, I told them I would see them the next class. They were all chattering about the exercise as they gathered their knapsacks and left the classroom.

Workshop #3: I placed an old tattered suitcase in the middle of the circle. It was from another time. I asked, "Who do you think that this suitcase belonged to? You cannot open it up. Just imagine where it has been or where it is going."

Each student was given paper and was asked to create an imaginary story about this suitcase. When they were done, we shared their writing. "See you tomorrow," I said. Again, the students left in great anticipation.

Workshop #4: The next day, when the students entered the drama room, the suitcase greeted them with a note taped to its side: OPEN ME. One of the students approached it and undid the clasps. The suitcase was filled with many artifacts, and numerous articles about the Holocaust. "Each of you is to choose one article and after you have finished, please select one artifact from the suitcase." There was an old silver wine cup, a child's painting, a prayer book, a yellow Star of David, a woman's shoe, a bar of soap, a letter, a passport, a photo of a family, a candlestick.

I then asked the students to speak as the artifact. We went around the circle listening to each student improvise the background of their artifact. They were trying to piece together the story of the suitcase. I told them that I would see them the next day. They left in great excitement.

Workshop #5: In the center of the room was a copy of Anne Frank's diary and 10 excerpts from it. Also, there were articles about Anne Frank, her history, and pictures of Anne and her family and the people who hid in the secret annex. "Read the articles and share the information with one other. Select an excerpt and return to the space that you sat in for workshop #1 and silently read your excerpt. Return to the circle. Read this excerpt aloud to the class."

Ten minutes before the end of the class, I gave each student a copy of the play that we would be studying and performing: *The Diary of Anne Frank*. There was quite the buzz. "Who's Anne? What part do I have?" I replied: "Open your plays to the *dramatis personae*. Your part is highlighted. Go home and read the play over the weekend and we will begin our work on Monday."

The students cheered when they discovered what role they had and told each other their parts. No one complained, no one was disappointed. They understood, as I did, that the right person had the right role and from that moment embraced their characters.

Final words of the week: "We are performing a play about a specific period in history where people hid to be safe. This is a story about hiding because of injustice and prejudice, but it is also about hope and human resilience. As we rehearse, many people in many parts of the world are in hiding so this play resonates the same horrible atrocities that they are enduring."

Let me tell you a little about the students who played these roles (note that students' names and countries have been changed to protect their privacy):

Mr. Frank: Khoi from Viet Nam
Mrs. Frank: Amy S. from Portugal
Anne Frank: Amy Y., Caucasian from Canada
Margot Frank: Chrisula from Cyprus
Mr. Van Daan: Jonathan from Portugal
Mrs. Van Daan: Maria from El Salvador
Peter Van Daan: Luis from Mexico
Mr. Dussel (we didn't have enough boys, so Mister became Miss)
    Tamara from mixed-race South Africa
Miep: Krystal, Caucasian from Canada
Mr. Kraler (became Mrs. Kraler): Elena from Bosnia

We began our work. Every day was exciting. Discoveries were made and oh what learning and what progress! Soon we were off script. They questioned the meaning behind the words. I reminded them: "Your challenge is to find the essence of the characters—who they were, their spirit, the very core that made them unique. The audience must know your character, not your color, not the shape of your eyes but the heart and nature of the person that you are honoring."

We worked hard. I remember rehearsing Act 11, Scene 3 where Miep arrives at night to let everyone know about the wonderful news of D-Day. There is great jubilation. Peter marches around banging on a frying pan, followed by Anne and Margot who give out flowers that they received from Miep.

"This is a time to celebrate!" announces Mr. Frank. He gets the cognac and a glass and Mr. Dussel fills it. He then raises his glass. "Here! Here! Schnapps! Locheim!" Khoi was playing the role of Mr. Frank. He had a dignity that Mr. Frank must have possessed. When Khoi came to this line, I helped him understand the significance of the gesture and I asked him to add its translation, "To life!" The cast worked this scene until it was perfect.

The dress rehearsal was scheduled for the morning before the evening performance. I had arranged for the cast to have the day off from classes. We spent the morning walking through lines; making adjustments to the set, props, costumes and lighting; making sure the timing was right for scene changes; and paying attention to scenes that needed some extra work. Dress rehearsal continued after lunch. I was relieved and hopeful. These students were so prepared, so in character, and so committed. They had grown beyond my expectations. They had not only become a solid cast but like the family they were portraying, they had become a family, a drama family.

When the rehearsal was over, we stayed on stage to talk and to have some down time. The set for this play was an interpretation of the secret annex that Anne Frank and her family, the Van Daan family, and Mr. Dussel had lived in. A sofa, some beds, and chairs were arranged on stage. This theatre set had become a serious space to rehearse in and a comfortable place to hang out in; a place to eat, talk, laugh, vent, nap, and finish homework; a living room for "our family."

We knew that this was going to be the last time together in this kind of environment. I delivered my director's notes and the cast discussed their concerns and made suggestions. They felt confident that their performance that evening would be a success. And then the conversation changed to who would be coming to the show. All the students' parents would be attending even if some of them didn't speak or understand English.

Stretched out beside one another, I realized how comfortable everyone was with each other. And then Elena began to speak. "Remember our first day of class when Mrs. Getz asked us to find a space of our own? We were not to leave it and had to remain silent for the whole period? When we began to rehearse, she told us that this play not only documents this historical time but honors those who have suffered injustices as well as those who are currently undergoing inhumane treatment. Well, I want to tell you, that I am one of those people who had to hide in order to save myself." I interrupted Elena because she had already told me her story and I remembered that she had wanted to keep it private and safe. I wanted to warn her to be sure about revealing it to us. She insisted, "I want to tell you so this play and the people who you are portraying will have true relevance. I think that if you know about this, it will help our performance and our play." I asked the cast to listen and to promise that what they were about to hear would stay in our special place. Elena told of her country's unrest and the political coup and how the rebels overtook the government. She took a deep breath and then told of the horror of watching as her father and uncle were executed. She spoke of the kind nuns who rescued Elena and her sister and hid them in the church attic for months. When she finished, she was not crying or shaking but remarkably calm. She had never told her story to anyone but me but now she felt relieved and proud and was quickly reassured that it would remain safe with us. The cast surrounded her, hugging her, comforting her. They thanked her for trusting them, for her brave spirit, and for her wisdom to share this remarkable experience. We saw Elena with new eyes.

Khoi shyly spoke up. "Well, I have a story, too. Although it's not as bad as Elena's. When I was five, I had to hide with my family in the jungle near my village in Viet Nam. My father was under suspicion by the government and he had found out that they were after him. When he arrived home, he shouted at us to gather a few things and told us that we had to leave immediately. We ran and ran as fast as we could, my mother, my sister and brother, my father and me. We had to leave our dog at home. We stayed for a few weeks in the dark jungle. My dad left for a few hours each to day to bring us food and water. I was so frightened." A sigh of compassion filled the stage.

"I ran, too," Maria bravely began. My mother and I left El Salvador in the middle of the night. If we crossed the border without being caught, we would be free, could get to Canada and then declare refugee status. During the night, we hid from soldiers and the lights of their trucks. I was so nervous that we would be caught but we made it. When safe on the other side, my mother made contact with her sister in California and my aunt arranged for our travel to her home. I was 12, the same age as Anne Frank. We stayed with my aunt for two years. My mom worked so hard and when she had saved enough money, we moved to Toronto."

I was numb and completely overwhelmed by my students' stories and by their resilience. I tried to be light-hearted and asked, "Anyone else to tell a story?" To my disbelief, Tamara whispered, "I do." She began to shake a little. "You don't have to tell, Tamara. "It's O.K. to keep it to yourself." But a sense of urgency took over. Tamara was from South Africa. Because she was of mixed race, she had been ostracized by the whites for being too black and when the blacks gained their freedom, she was seen as too white and therefore became the enemy. One afternoon, three soldiers broke into her home. She was there with her older sister. Tamara was 13 and her sister, 15. By luck and speed, Tamara ran into her room and quickly hid inside her closet but her sister was not as fortunate. The soldiers raped her while Tamara shook in terror.

Complete and utter silence fell upon our set. Four students, four beautiful children had endured such traumas. Yet here they stood, so bright, so brave, so vulnerable, filled with hope, ready to perform a play that ironically echoed their stories. They were waiting for me to break this painful silence. I looked at them and said, "I don't have any words. I am at a loss. There are no words that can justify the magnitude of your experiences." "Yes there are!" Khoi's firm voice was heard. "There are two words," he replied with a smile, taking his time to look at each of us. "Locheim—to life." We all gathered in the center of Anne Frank's set and raised our glasses together.

6

Remaining Hopeful

Anyone who knows me well and has visited the various classrooms and offices that I have occupied over the course of my career knows that I am something of a packrat. I keep too many things. Quotes, books, pieces of student writing, articles, papers, letters and other artifacts, images, cartoons, and poems are all over the place. I am loath to throw them away in case I need them for something—a class, a presentation, or an idea to enhance an article.

When I began to write this book, I was moving offices at York University and a quote fell out of an old poetry anthology that I had bought when I was a university student—about 40 years ago. The quote was from *The Life of Samuel Johnson* by James Boswell, a text that was required reading in a first-year English course. Obviously I had scribbled the words on a piece of paper because they had had some kind of impact on me. The quote seemed to be saying, "Now is your time to use me!"

Johnson described the "cold reserve too common among Englishmen to strangers." He condemned his countrymen for their reticence in getting to know each other: "Two Englishmen, shown into a room together at a house where they are both visitors, would probably go each to a different window, and remain in obstinate silence. Sir, we as yet do not understand the common rights of humanity."

This image of two individuals not wanting to connect, not willing to interact, not caring about each other's story has stayed with me. I don't want us—here in the twenty-first century—to "go each to a different window" and I don't want our students to do that, either. I want classrooms to be places where students are genuinely engaged not only with the curriculum but also with each other. I want schools to be places where students meet, get to know one another, and rejoice in how their individual stories intersect and diverge. I want their stories to be told in the right circumstances for the right reasons. "Learning to read oneself is also about learning to read the other," says John Willinsky. And learning to read each other will allow our students to read the world as they grow up.

Another one of my treasures is an old copy of a *New Yorker* magazine that I have kept for a number of years. On the front cover is a cartoon sketch of a subway car that has been transformed into a beautiful, old-fashioned reading room. There is a long oak desk with many of those wonderful reading lamps made of bronze with shiny green shades. Passengers are sitting comfortably enjoying a book or a newspaper.

If only our classrooms could be like that. Everyone would be warm and have a seat. All learners would be assured of a destination. Students would be comforted by the opportunities that are depicted in the subway ads. The environment would be aesthetic as well as utilitarian. There would be a coziness and a beauty that encourages them to embrace learning. There would be a sense of moving forward.

I have always been interested in helping disengaged students become engaged in school. I am worried about decreasing opportunities for the poor and the disenfranchised who are dragged down by the dynamics of the global economy. I feel a responsibility to those students who struggle to learn in an environment where high-stakes testing seems to be more important than it should be. I am aware of the urgent need to make schools safe places for learning and of the importance of finding ways to connect what needs to be taught to what has to be learned.

School is not a rehearsal space. It is a "now" space that must provide students with the knowledge, skills, attitudes, and values they need to live in the present while preparing themselves for the future. Teachers play an enormous role in developing flexible frames of mind and maintaining hope in their students' hearts. Teachers must maintain high expectations for all students and withhold judgement to allow their students to blossom in their own time.

Dylan Williams' research on assessment and evaluation (1998) emphasizes that frequent and specific feedback—assessment for learning—is essential to student achievement. He states that teachers need to *increase* descriptive, specific feedback and *decrease* evaluative feedback. In other words, we need to tell our students what they are doing well and what they need to work on rather than constantly marking their work, judging them, and telling them what they have done wrong.

Deciding What to Hope For

Seventeenth-century playwright Jean-Baptise Molière once wrote: "We are responsible not only for what we do but also for what we do not do." The work that is done in anti-discriminatory teaching is difficult and often uncomfortable. Sometimes it just seems easier to ignore injustice and keep teaching traditional material in traditional ways. But in truth, as I hope this book has demonstrated, this is not the way that fairness works. Differences—of opinion, insight, experience, and perspectives—need to be named and acknowledged. Failing to do this just perpetuates inequality and unequal relations (as Ratna Ghosh, a professor and former Dean of Education at McGill University, points out). It is important to confront the challenges head-on: to take the risks involved in talking about difficult issues and to find powerful ways to explore the layers of meaning, the ambiguities, and the various perspectives from the inside out. As Codi's sister, Hallie (a teacher who chooses to teach in Central America) states in Barbara Kingsolver's novel *Animal Dreams*: "Good things don't get lost." In her letter to her sister, Hallie writes:

> Codi, here's what I've decided: the very least you can do in your life is to figure out what you hope for. Not admire it from a distance but live right in it,

The future isn't something hidden in a corner. The future is something we build in the present.

Paulo Freire

under its roof. What I want is so simple I almost can't say it: elementary kindness. Enough to eat, enough to go around. The possibility that kids might one day grow up to be neither the destroyers, nor the destroyed. That's about it. Right now I'm living in that hope, running down its hallway and touching the walls on both sides.

Barbara Kingsolver. *Animal Dreams*, p. 299

Professional Learning Communities

How do we stay hopeful in difficult times? How do we make sure that the good things we do on a regular basis with our students don't get lost? How do we keep our confidence and vision concerning equitable classrooms alive? It is important to help students and teachers realize that it is not our differences that divide us but rather our judgements about each other. It is also vitally important to keep talking to one another: student to student, teacher to teacher, student to teacher, teacher to administrator, family member to teacher, and so on. We must make sure we are supported by each other as we do this difficult work. In her book, *Turning to One Another: Simple Conversations to Restore Hope to the Future,* Margaret Wheatley writes about conversations being essentially the "practice of freedom":

> As we think together, as we question things, as we are stirred to act to change things, we exercise our innate right to be free. Paulo Freire described love as "an act of courage, not of fear." When we find the courage to approach those we fear, that is a gesture of love…. So freedom and love are intimately related. When our actions create freedom for ourselves and others, that too is a gesture of love.

Shining Threads of Hope

I am often asked to speak at Educational Leadership conferences about collaborative leadership and maintaining hope in difficult circumstances. These speeches grew out of a presentation I gave in 1995 to the delegates at the Toronto Principals' Association. The year before, the Association chair had asked me to address the conference on the topic of "wellness." I felt awkward because wellness was not and still is not my area of expertise. I did not know how to begin to prepare. Then, suddenly and tragically, the speech was canceled because a vice-principal and a guidance teacher were wounded in a school shooting the day before the conference was to take place. Everyone was in shock. As a result, the speech on wellness was postponed until the following year. However, the event and various ideas swirled around in my mind for a year. Ideas about violence, safety in schools, students' sense of self, teachers' sense of students, inclusionary practices, leadership, and wellness evolved into a speech that I called "Shining Threads of Hope."

In the speech, I reminded the audience that we need to be aware of the context in which we are living and teaching and the rapid change that is happening on a daily basis. We need to rely upon the community of teachers, parents and guardians, and other staff with whom we work so that we can offer an education that is fair for all. We need to be aware of what we can control and rely upon our imaginations and the success stories of others to help us see that we are not alone. And, finally, we need to connect with that special someone with whom we can be very honest and who can guide us toward doing the right thing for the right reasons.

The Context in Which We Live and Teach

We all know that we are living in times of enormous change, not only in education but also in every aspect of society. Our global economy allows jobs to be moved to wherever wages are lowest; computer technology has replaced millions of workers; and transnational corporations play cities, states, and increasingly whole countries off against each other, thus influencing taxation and fiscal policies. All of this change affects homes and businesses everywhere in the world. Homes mean families and families mean students and students mean us: teachers, administrators, and leaders in education who have to manage change that is often hard to detect. Not only is change more rapid than it has ever been, but also the pressure on all of us to succeed and to be accountable despite the change is greater than it has ever been. In the province in which I teach, we have tests at Grades 3, 6, and 10. Tests create insecurity in this changing world and insecurity is at an all-time high.

Given this context, how do we move ahead *and remain hopeful in times of change?*

Michael Fullan, an expert on educational change, tells us that it is essential to be hopeful, especially when things are not. He talks about "active hope": how important it is to continue believing that one own's efforts really can make a difference (2001). The Toronto Board of Education's trucks used to have the following motto written on them in large letters: *Toronto teachers make a difference.* We have to remember that what we do every day as teachers *does* have an impact. We make a difference in the lives of our students by *how* and *what* we teach.

I remember working in an elementary school at the time that a new report card was being piloted in the schools. Each student had to make a comment at the end of the report card as a personal assessment of their progress. The principal, Kaye Davies, a friend of mine with whom I had worked steadily for many years and who had helped me implement drama-in-education in the Toronto elementary schools, asked me to drop into her office before I left. "I have a present for you," she said. When I arrived, she handed me a copy of a Grade 4 report card—with the student's name blacked out. The student had written:

> What I do good in is my art and drama because they give me a sense of control in this world of chaos.

This 9-year-old knew what Michael Fullan knows and has articulated in *Rethinking Educational Change with Heart and Mind* (1997). "Hope," Fullan says, "is not a sunny view of life. It is the capacity not to panic in tight situations and to find ways and resources to address difficult problems." Fullan insists that schools will flourish if there is a high level of trust and support amongst colleagues.

Collaboration Versus Competition

Collaboration is important. What I have learned while working with teachers and administrators over the years is that people only support what they create together. *People don't resist change; they resist being changed.* We have to find a way for educators to buy in to new ideas—to help them see the worth of new ideas in terms of their own teaching and the success of their students. If we are intent on implementing inclusive practices in schools, we need to build leadership capacity that is lasting. Leadership capacity must be built on a clear vision and it must be founded upon the rich data compiled in contemporary research. As well, these efforts need to honor everyone in the school and they must be collaborative rather than competitive. If I chair a meeting, I resist setting up situations in which teachers share only their success stories. Sometimes I find that inviting people to tell others about their struggles and disappointments binds us together even more than stories of success. Sharing our sorrows and concerns makes us very competent healers. Perhaps we should ask our colleagues:

- What was your biggest challenge in teaching this material?
- What did you do and to whom did you turn for help when you encountered resistance?
- How did you deal with disappointments along the way?
- What help would you offer teachers who are going to try to teach this way?
- What resources do you wish you had on hand?
- Where can we go from here?

Collegiality

I have also discovered that you have to rely upon others as well as yourself in order to make the kind of pedagogical change that is needed to teach inclusively. You cannot do this alone. You need to talk things out, co-teach, reflect on your strategies after the fact, and go back into the classroom with new ideas.

> Remember the story of the farmer boy whose cow gave birth to a little calf? Every day the boy would carry the calf up the mountain to the pasture and return with it in the evening. At first, the little animal weighed only fifty pounds but every day the calf gained a pound or two—an inconsequential amount, of course, and an increment the boy could easily bear. As the calf grew into a cow, the boy continued to carry it up the mountain, despite its weight of 1500 pounds. It was an extraordinary load but because the boy had been carrying the calf from its infancy, and because each daily increment was small, it was possible for him to carry an animal ten times his own weight up the mountain.
>
> Roland Barth

There is a "weight" to this kind of work that is connected to our moral obligations, to authenticity, to taking risks in order to teach about difficult issues—and we need to find allies as we move forward. The Elementary Teachers' Federation of Ontario defines Professional Learning Communities as "a group of education professionals who share common visions, values, and goals, and work collaboratively using inquiry, experimentation, and innovation to improve teaching and student learning."

The work toward inclusive education takes time, modeling, research, and many conversations—about practice, identity, philosophy, and perspectives.

What *Can* I Control?

I want to teach hard skills in soft ways and to mentor the new teachers who are coming into the system with fewer supports than I had when I began my career. When life seems to be out of control, I remind my student teachers that although they do not have control over *what* they must teach, they do have control about *how* they are going to teach it. I help them to become literate in terms of both assessment and pedagogy. I warn them that we all need to monitor our language and our assumptions on a regular basis. I can control and monitor the language that I use. For instance, I will not think of my students as "clients" or parents as "stakeholders." I will not talk about "bottom lines." I will not use these words—because they remind me of a competitive, non-compassionate environment that I do not wish to see emulated in my classrooms.

Constructing Together

The work in anti-discriminatory education is intense. The context is difficult. The effort we have to exert to get everyone on board is huge. Roland Barth reminds us that the function of schools is:

To make learning focused and efficient

To present ideas that people would be unlikely to stumble over

To look after each other

These goals are especially tough for those of us in public education who must always maintain an outwardly positive attitude and appear to enjoy doing more with less. I think we have to find someone amongst our associates with whom we can be really honest, someone who will listen to us complain, let us talk about it, and never, ever tell. I advise my teacher candidates to find a friend who doesn't always advise you to look on the bright side of things. It is important to find that person who allows sorrow to be shared so that healing can take place and teaching fairly can continue.

As we move forward, we must watch carefully and respond to what we see working and seek a forum to make changes for the better. In the end, we have to decide what to hope for and have the courage to keep that vision alive. We must concentrate on the moments that bring us joy—record them, tell the stories, laugh, and cry. I am about to embark on an exciting adventure of storytelling with teachers from Alberta. Twelve teachers, three musicians, and I will be creating a storytelling anthology to be performed at an educational conference in 2009. The teachers will come together to talk about what keeps them teaching despite the difficult circumstances they face every day. We'll explore questions such as: What are the reasons we became teachers? What are the compelling reasons for staying in this profession?

In this book, I hope that I have given teachers some viable ideas about how to lend social, emotional, and intellectual support to their students, how to maintain high expectations for all students, how to take the time to acknowledge who their students are and where they are from, and how to tailor instructional strategies to meet the needs of all students so that they provide them with learning experiences that are relevant, open-ended, imaginative, thought-provoking, and challenging. I hope that teachers will pick and choose from the ideas presented in this book, and extend, adapt, and experiment with those activities that might work well and set aside those that might not be appropriate in certain teaching and learning contexts. I also hope that teachers will scaffold the activities in such a way that the work in the classroom does not become "tinny and dishonest' but rather thoughtful, engaging, and transformative on many levels. I hope that teachers will gradually become more comfortable working from the "inside out."

Martha Nussbaum, the Ernst Freund Distinguished Service Professor of Law and Ethics at the University of Chicago, has taught us that arts in the classroom help us create "a more generous view of the ways that we come to know ourselves." Drama certainly has an amazing capability—to let us enter into another's world, move around within it for a while, "try on roles," experience relationships, uncover new meanings in conversations, and, ultimately, rethink our perceptions of the way in which we want to live in the world. The work that we do in the classroom is not easy. It requires us to be spontaneous, to put our trust in one another, and to have faith that we will gain a gradual understanding of each other as members of a community striving to make meaning together.

Whenever we try to understand other human beings, there is always the risk that misunderstandings will occur. Whenever we ask students to pay attention to nuance and detail, our differences in perception come to the fore. Whenever we delve into subtexts, we find that our own histories and the way in which we see the world lead us to different interpretations and inferences. This is what makes the work in the classroom so challenging. It is also what makes the teaching and learning dynamic so important. Maxine Greene reminds us that the teacher's role is to be "open to the wonder" of being in the classroom. Teachers, she says, are the agents who can "light the slow fuse of possibility even for the defeated ones, the bored ones, the deserted ones. There is room for them; we can make room for them in our community of recognition, wide-awakeness, caring and regard."

The teachers and students who have been part of my life for over thirty-three years of teaching have taught me more than I have ever taught them. They have allowed me to take risks in their classrooms and we have spent long hours deconstructing what happened and preparing for new ventures together. I continue to make mistakes as I do this work. The students and teachers have been patient and respectful as we change direction and start again from different vantage points. They know that I am enormously self-critical when I make mistakes but I have finally learned to let forgiveness seep in. Forgiveness gives me the courage to keep going.

Many years ago, I gave a speech to a group of Special Education teachers and lost my bearings. Afterwards, one of the teachers in the audience wrote me a note that included a poem based on "The Paradoxical Commandments" below. She said that she knew what I was trying to say but that I needed to rephrase my words. "Keep going," she said. "The work is important—crucial to the safety of our kids and to the future of the world." So, I will leave my readers with the thoughts that this forgiving teacher shared with me as an incentive to keep going, be strong, be brave, and continue to polish those shining threads of hope so that we can all continue to teach fairly in an unfair world.

The Paradoxical Commandments
By Kent M. Keith

1. People are illogical, unreasonable, and self-centered.
   Love them anyway.

2. If you do good, people will accuse you of selfish ulterior motives.
   Do good anyway.

3. If you are successful, you will win false friends and true enemies.
   Succeed anyway.

4. The good you do today will be forgotten tomorrow.
   Do good anyway.

5. Honesty and frankness make you vulnerable.
   Be honest and frank anyway.

6. The biggest men and women with the biggest ideas can be shot down by the smallest men and women with the smallest minds.
   Think big anyway.

7. People favor underdogs but follow only top dogs.
   Fight for a few underdogs anyway.

8. What you spend years building may be destroyed overnight.
   Build anyway.

9. People really need help but may attack you if you do help them.
   Help people anyway.

10. Give the world the best you have and you'll get kicked in the teeth.
    Give the world the best you have anyway.

© Copyright Kent M. Keith 1968, Renewed, 2001
The Paradoxical Commandments were written by Kent M. Keith as part of his book, **The Silent Revolution: Dynamic Leadership in the Student Council**, published in 1968 by Harvard Student Agencies, Cambridge, Massachusetts.

---

50 Teaching Strategies to Use in an Inclusive Classroom

1. I Am From… / We Are From…

Students record reflections in writing about where they are from (in terms of their identities) in response to various kinds of prompts from the teacher. They then share their writing with a partner. Finally, they combine their writing to create a "We are from…" poem that they present to the class through voice and movement.

2. Lay Your Cards on the Table

In this exercise, participants create personal cards describing their various identities related to their present circumstances. They talk about their identities in small groups—laying only those cards on the table that they feel comfortable talking about. This strategy allows students to discuss inclusion and exclusion from a personal perspective.

3. Cooperative Games

Cooperative games are an excellent way to set up learning communities in which everyone feels connected to each other and in which students strive to achieve a common goal. Participants learn to be aware of how to include everyone in the class in efforts to achieve collective success. Cooperative games forge friendships and connections that eventually allow classrooms to become "communities of conscience." Students learn to identify who is involved in the classroom dynamic, who has "shut down," who is feeling excluded, and who is gaining confidence.

4. Name Games

These are a series of games in which participants have fun learning the names of classmates and how to pronounce them. (For examples, see pages 38–41 in this book.)

5. The Expert Game

This exercise lets students pose critical questions in a context that elicits oral language and facilitates social interaction. Ask students to get into groups of five or six. Have them number themselves off. Student number 1 will be interviewed for a job in role as an expert in his or her field: a criminal lawyer, a social worker who works with homeless people, a 911 operator, and so on. The members of the interview team decide on the qualities and skills the expert needs to have and they collaborate to create some introductory questions. Tell the experts in a private conversation that they are to pretend to know as much as possible about their area of expertise. Encourage them to use their imaginations and to take their role seriously. Send the experts back to their groups. Say, "On my signal, I want you to begin the interview." Invite the candidate to sit down for the interview. Allow the interview to last three or four minutes and then ask one of the interviewers some questions, for example: "At this point in the interview, what is your overall impression of the candidate? Are you leaning towards hiring this individual? Why or why not? What further questions would you like to ask before you make your decision?" Everyone in the group should have a chance to play the role of an expert.

6. Designing Miniature Sets

Building miniature sets for stories or plays gives students a chance to work collaboratively with the architectural, symbolic, and metaphorical aspects of the narratives they are studying or creating. They work together in small groups to create a miniature set that includes a number of artifacts (for example, rocking chairs and broken windows) that have layered meanings.

7. Collaborative Art Installation

Once students have created pieces of art based on a theme, have them arrange them in a wide-open space. Ask everyone to remain silent as individual students rearrange the pieces of art so that they convey some sort of message or are pleasing to the eye. You might wish to play some soft music to accompany this exercise. Everyone should have an opportunity to manipulate the images. There is no right or wrong arrangement of the artwork.

8. Statues

Have individual students mimic a statue that represents an image from a story that they found memorable and to which they feel connected. Have them bring their statues alive for three seconds and then freeze in another position. If you add music, the exercise will resemble a silent movie.

9. Sculpture Garden

Groups of students create tableaux that involve a common character from a story. After the scenes have been created, have everyone in all the tableaux move to the sides of the classroom, leaving the central character in each group in his or her position as a statue. Read poetry or play music and have students rearrange the statues as if they were in some kind of sculpture garden or gallery. Classmates can whisper in each statue's ear and have the person move to another part of the room or move closer to other statues.

10. Four Times Story Nouns

Distribute a copy of a very simple story to students. Ask the students to get into groups of four and to underline all the nouns in the story. Next, have them find three synonyms for each noun using thesauruses and dictionaries. Have them create an expanded story and devise a way to read it as a whole class.

11. Role-Playing

Students adopt a role and enter into a story or a character's life, learning about the character's feelings and motivations vicariously through that experience, and then emerge with a new understanding of another person's reality. Students in role take on new voices and new perspectives, and reflect on the experience afterwards by writing in role about their new insights and deepened understanding.

12. Interviewing in Role

Students in role are interviewed by other students playing the role of reporters (as an example), who ask questions about their motives, decisions, beliefs, and values. The students then go "out of role" and talk about their new understandings of people and events.

13. Writing in Role

Writing in role occurs when students who have been involved in a role-playing situation write from the perspective of the character that they portrayed. Often the writing is surprisingly good because students have "lived through" a dramatic moment and can write about their physical, emotional, and intellectual involvement in an imagined situation. As a result, they are not only inside the story but also inside the language of the story. Their responses are immediate and visceral. Thinking and speaking in the role of the character allows students to use vocabulary and turns of phrase that they do not generally use when they speak as themselves. They experiment with new language forms and registers and are therefore more adept at writing down what they have already thought and spoken out loud. Writing in role can take many form: reports, diaries, obituaries, signs, proclamations, affidavits, secret messages in code, cartoons, CD images and titles, poems, letters, tombstone engravings, court documents, announcements, and so on.

14. If Pictures Could Move

In groups of four, students focus on a page in a graphic novel that they are reading. The page must feature two or more of the following elements: at least three characters, captions, sound effects, whisper bubbles, speech bubbles, and thought bubbles. Students work to re-create the panels, bringing the language in the speech and thought bubbles to life and demonstrating the movement from panel to panel while at the same time devising appropriate sound effects. They attempt to represent as precisely as possible the images and words portrayed in a particular section of the novel. A narrator can read the captions, other students can add sound effects, and other students can read the language in the speech and thought bubbles. Let the students experiment with different kinds of voices and movements. When one frame ends, have students use a signal, such as a drumbeat, to indicate that the story has moved to the next panel. Each group can share its work with another group in the class.

15. If Pictures Could Talk

Display an image of one or more people using an overhead projector. Ensure that the image is intriguing so that students are curious to know more about what the person or people are thinking and feeling in the picture. Individually, have students write about what they see in the picture, what memories it conjures, and what they imagine is happening in the picture. Then have the students work with a partner to reach agreement on what is taking place in the picture. Have them write a title or caption for the visual on a piece of paper. Then distribute cutout speech bubbles, thought bubbles, and whisper bubbles and have the students create bubbles to match the caption. Have them present their talking pictures to another set of partners.

16. Bursting the Bubble

Have students look closely at the ways in which the artist has portrayed the characters in a graphic novel. What does a character's body language tell the reader about the character? What do the characters' gestures tell us? How does a character's posture convey an instant message? (Do characters seem nervous, protective, confident, aggressive, stand-offish, at ease, frightened?) After students have discussed the ways in which the images communicate information about the characters, have the students enlarge each speech bubble or "burst it" so that classmates can hear more about what each character is thinking, feeling, and wondering about. Have students write in role as the characters and then share their writing with a partner or in small groups.

17. Chamber Theatre

In small groups, students create a scene from a story and then freeze. Other students from the class come and stand by each actor and speak his or her thoughts in role. Volunteers are encouraged to provide multiple perspectives in role. Discussion follows.

18. Storytelling in Small Groups

A group of students who have read the same text or who have listened to the same story number off. On a prearranged signal, student number 1 from each group begins retelling the story until the signal sounds. Students number 2 take over the retelling, followed by students number 3, and so on. You may wish to have students pass along a pencil or an artifact of some sort as they retell the story; the artifact might be a key, a collar of a dress, a medal that was once pinned on a uniform, and so on.

19. Role on the Wall

On the chalkboard or chart paper, a volunteer draws a large abstract outline of a character that appears in a story that the class is reading. The figure should be large enough so that students can write descriptive words and phrases inside it. The name of the character is written within the figure. Inside the figure as well, class members write as many words as possible to describe the person's psychological, emotional, and physical characteristics. In the space immediately surrounding the figure, they write the names of people or things that support the person. Farther away from the figure, students write words that describe the difficulties facing the person. The students watch as the figure fills up with words. Play music in the background and have two or three people at a time record their thoughts. After everyone has had a chance to contribute some words, conduct a whole-class discussion about the words generated.

20. Modeled Reading

In modeled reading situations, teachers demonstrate reading strategies by sharing the reading process with students. They read aloud to students to show, demonstrate, explain, instruct, and interpret their own thinking processes while reading. Students watch, engage, listen, follow along, share ideas, ask questions, and participate in the discussion that follows.

21. Inner/Outer Circle; Reading Our Writing

Divide the students into two groups. One group forms a circle representing one of the characters from a story that the class has been investigating. The other group forms a circle around those students representing another character who has a different perspective on an issue compared to the first character. The teacher calls upon the students to share, in role, their inner thoughts and feelings. Students may speak spontaneously or read from writing that they have written in role. The teacher acts as an orchestra leader, juxtaposing voices and genres to create a theatrical reading illustrating various perspectives

22. Map-Making

Students work in groups to create a map of the setting of a novel, newspaper article, poem, or play that they are reading. They become acquainted with the physical characteristics of the setting of the text so they can visualize the characters and their contexts more clearly as they read and explore the material.

23. Making and Working With Lists

I use a lot of index cards when I teach. There is something about index cards that seems to set students free in their writing. A large piece of paper makes those students who worry about writing even more anxious about the length of the written piece that will be required. Often I begin a class by asking the students to write a list. I tell them that they will understand more about the purpose of the list as our work together progresses. They are happy to wonder about the list's purpose as I dictate items to them. We then work with the list, prioritizing items and discussing our reasons for choosing them.

24. Creating Critical Questions

Students are asked to create questions that will help them understand a story's characters, relationships, context, setting, and central problem better as they explore texts and situations in small groups. For instance, if they have read an excerpt from a novel, they write down everything they know for sure based on what they have read. They then pose critical questions about what they don't know, what they want to know, and who could help them find answers to their questions.

25. Voiceover Narration

The teacher narrates the actions in a scene while a group of students listens and responds in different ways, through movement or tableaux, for example. This strategy allows teachers to consolidate information and student responses or to create a transitional bridge in their teaching as they move on to another activity.

26. Moving to Words: Flocking

Flocking is a form of spontaneous movement improvisation. A group works collectively as students shift position, sometimes following, sometimes leading one another's movements. Flocking can be used with three or more people to investigate a theme, image, character, concept, or journey.

First, students number themselves off in small groups and organize themselves in a diamond formation. Student number 1 acts as the first leader and faces a wall or a window; the other students face the same way. When student number 1 begins to move, the other students shadow or mirror the movement. After a while, student number 1, as leader, rotates to the right and the other students follow the rotation so that they are now following student number 2, who initiates the movement that the others shadow. Student number 3 then initiates the movement; and finally, student number 4 does so.

The students move to music. It is best to choose slow music so that the movement can be sustained and the groups can follow one another and make easy transitions. Encourage students to experiment with different kinds of movement, changing tempo, style, and energy level. If they are focused on representing a theme through their movements, the words that they choose can relate to one another or they can be juxtaposed to create a sense of dissonance.

27. The Wave

This movement exercise relies on a group's ability to work together and communicate non-verbally. It involves up to eight students walking in unison, shoulder to shoulder, and then spontaneously dropping out of the line to create statues or shapes that reflect the characters, themes, and emotions being explored. The exercise is beautiful to watch.

Divide the class into groups of six to eight. While one group creates the Wave, the others stand on both sides of the space to watch and reflect on the experience. Everyone has a chance to participate.

The working group stands at one end of the room. I encourage them to stand shoulder to shoulder in a straight line, almost touching elbows.

On my signal, the group moves forward simultaneously, crosses the room, turns around, and returns—the students all the while maintaining a close, straight formation. I encourage them to "sense each other's impulses" as they walk together.

The next step is to create statues. As the group crosses the room the second time, anyone can spontaneously "fall out" of the line and create a statue or shape that represents the character's feelings, thoughts, or reactions. The other students keep walking. When the walkers turn around and come back, they bring the statue back into the line. As they gain more confidence and skill at this exercise, students playing statues can wait for one or more Waves before being brought back into the line—doing so allows the onlookers more time to observe the statues. If you wish, you can play music during the exercise.

28. Modeled Writing

The teacher acts as a scribe in front of the class, writing on the chalkboard while thinking aloud. She or he models the way in which authentic writers write—going back over a draft, rereading it out loud, crossing out or erasing what does not sound right, adding words and phrases, and moving chunks of text around. The students observe the think-aloud and offer suggestions for improving the teacher's written piece.

29. Voices in the Head

This activity allows students to reflect upon the complexity of the material they are studying, especially if it involves a character who is living through a difficult time and who must make a life-altering decision. One student role-plays that character and other students act as that person's collective conscience by offering the character advice.

30. Brainstorming

Brainstorming allows groups of students to generate a "pool" of ideas, examples, and questions without fear of criticism. A recorder is appointed and all ideas are written down. Later, groups will work with the material to explore a topic or idea in greater depth. Students can expand on one another's ideas, ask questions, enter into debate about the worth of an idea, and suggest alternatives. However, during the brainstorming session, students should simply generate any and all ideas and write them down. No negative responses or editing are allowed.

31. Hieroglyphics

Hieroglyphics give students an opportunity to make meaning by organizing a series of symbols. They can create a powerful story by arranging symbols in a particular sequence and then interpreting the story through movement.

32. Spontaneous Improvisation in Small Groups

Students spontaneously act out a given situation—improvising the who, where, what, when, and why of a predicament confronting the characters in a narrative. They create an unscripted scene that allows the class to examine one group's interpretation of what is being studied in class.

33. Using Artifacts

Introduce artifacts at strategic points in your lessons to "hook" students into wondering about things and encouraging them to ask questions. I use artifacts to introduce historical events, to help students make their way through difficult texts, to find common connections with their classmates, and to inspire discussion and debate. Students love to pass artifacts around a circle in small groups, wondering about their use or origin, linking them to the characters and incidents in the books and poetry that they are reading, and using them as props in their oral presentations to captivate their audience.

34. Story/Word Punctuation

Students pore over images in picture books and write down the words or phrases that come to mind. The teacher then reads the book and stands by the students, giving each student time to say their words or phrases out loud. The text and student responses are thus woven together in a new kind of oral reading.

35. Tableaux

Tableaux, or frozen images, are an excellent way of framing moments of significance that students encounter in their reading, writing, and discussions. These frozen pictures "bottle time" and allow students to demonstrate through their bodies (using facial expressions, gestures, positions, and movement) their understanding about what is being taught. Students appreciate "seeing" the text as well as reading it.

Explain to students that tableaux are still images or "freeze frames" of people who represent not just a moment in time, but also a *problem* in time. Encourage them to create images with their bodies that tell some kind of story. They can crystallize a key moment, idea, reaction, statement, or theme that the rest of the class as the audience can then study, analyze, and discuss.

Tableaux require that students work in groups to discuss, collaborate, and select an image that they want to represent and communicate something about. Students might get into groups of three to create tableaux such as Baby's First Step, An Unwanted Haircut, Vice-Principal's Office: Late Again?, First Day in a New School, or Freedom: The First Moment of Summer Vacation.

For the practice session, I ask one group to volunteer as demonstrators. Before working in groups, the whole class observes how effective the technique can be. I invite students to think about and experiment with:

- different levels of body positions—high, medium, low—so that the image is varied in form;
- various body shapes (open, closed) to make sure that the important elements in the tableau can be seen by the rest of the class when the tableau is shared;
- the relationships in terms of physical distance between and among characters in the tableau;
- what the audience will focus on when the image is frozen and analyzed; and
- different kinds of emotions, body language, and facial expressions that will communicate meaning effectively.

36. Stepping In and Out of Pictures

Once students have created tableaux in groups of three, I ask them to concentrate on bringing the frozen pictures to life. As a group shares an image, members step out of the picture one by one and speak lines of dialogue or improvise what the characters might say at that moment. They then step back into the picture and allow someone else to speak.

Often, I ask students in the audience to indicate which character they would like to address. The classmate approaches someone in the tableau and brings that character to life by asking a question. The rest of the students in the tableau remain frozen as the chosen character replies to the question.

37. Drawing and Writing

After a group has composed a tableau, have the other students do quick gesture drawings without lifting their pencils from the page. Can they find the implied movement in the image? Can they then work with what they have created to make the drawing into a composition about people and the different power relationships among them?

Deconstructing tableaux allows students to enter into a character's interior reality. It also teaches students that none of us perceives the same things in the same ways.

38. Teacher in Role

The teacher takes part in a drama along with the students by adopting a role. The teacher in role is able to work inside the situation, creating a climate in which the honesty of individual contributions is valued and respect is shown to everyone who contributes ideas. The teacher in role imbues the situation with seriousness of purpose and adds an element of creative tension to the work-in-progress.

39. Prepared Improvisation

Prepared improvisations are enactments of key moments that are central to a drama. Like tableaux, prepared improvisations require planning and collaboration. In order to be effective, the students must be selective about the moment they wish to enact and they need to use appropriate dialogue in the scene.

40. Parallel Universes

Students work in small groups to create contrasting tableaux or scenes of various characters that are being studied. They create "parallel universes" and juxtapose the activities and locations of different characters at precisely the same time. This activity allows the students to uncover different perspectives and gain an understanding of the irony of given situations.

41. Forum Theatre

A dramatic situation is improvised by a small group while the rest of the class observes. Then everyone has a chance to participate in creating the scene again, but this time, participants can stop the scene to make suggestions or take over a role. Forum theatre provides the class with an opportunity to explore a range of possible options, reactions, solutions, or outcomes associated with the drama. Students work together to shape an authentic scene and find ways to make it satisfying to viewers.

42. Rearranging the Pictures

Have students look closely at advertisements in magazines. Advertisers design ads strategically by composing the elements in the ad to generate certain effects. Often, advertisers overlay words to amplify an image to influence the reader. Have students play with the images, arranging and rearranging their elements. Have them analyze who is present and who is absent in the advertisement. What messages are being conveyed and to whom? Whose point of view does the message represent? Whose points of view are missing?

43. Hot-seating

Hot seating is an activity in which the students, performing as themselves, have an opportunity to question or interview a role-player who remains in character. The individual student sits in the "hot seat" at the front of the classroom and answers questions in role. I use this teaching strategy when I work with plays, novels, and historical incidents. I often help students prepare the kinds of questions they wish to ask before the person in role sits on the hot seat.

44. Split-Second Scenes

In order to understand a situation in greater depth, students act out a split-second scene for the rest of the class to analyze. The students might begin by composing a tableau and then bring it alive for 30 seconds or so.

45. Circular Drama

Groups create different scenes involving a central character. The teacher enters the scene in role and asks the characters in the scene probing questions to uncover various meanings.

46. This Is Your Line

Before viewing a play or a movie, place important lines from the script in individual envelopes with the name of each student on the outside of the envelope. A week before the viewing, instruct students to open their envelope and read the line to the class. While viewing the play or movie, the students wait to hear their line. Afterwards, they write a short paragraph about the significance of that line to them and its contribution to the play's or movie's meaning and overall effect.

47. Overheard Conversations

When students are involved in role-playing with partners or in small groups, the teacher, on a signal, asks everyone to freeze. The teacher then stands beside a group who continues their improvisation. In this way, students have an opportunity to listen in on what is being said in other groups.

48. Walk Around Reading

Have the students begin reading a text as they walk around the room. Tell them that when they reach the end of the text, they are to begin reading the text from the beginning again. Have them continue reading. Encourage them to listen to their classmates reading as they wander around the room. (You might want to stagger the reading so that not everyone is reading at the same time. Start people off by touching them gently on the shoulder. Make sure that you don't forget anybody.)

On an agreed-upon signal, have everyone stop reading and stand quietly. Ask the students to find their favorite line, phrase, or word in the text. Tell them that when you touch them gently on the shoulder, you want them to say their line, phrase, or word out loud.

Create a new oral reading by hearing these favorite words, lines, or phrases recited out loud by different voices in different ways.

49. Choral Speaking

Choral speaking and chanting involve experimentation, interpretation, and rehearsal of a piece of text, for example, a poem or a riddle. The students discuss the meaning of the text and consider who might be speaking and to whom. The group experiments with the language of the text, exploring rhythm, cadence, volume, and pace. Some parts of the text may be read solo and some in unison with either the whole group or part of the group.

50. Readers Theatre

Readers Theatre is a sophisticated form of choral reading. Students read aloud material in small groups, conveying a meaning of the material that is not normally meant for performance. The group members decide on focus, timing, pacing, roles, voice intonation, and pauses. They try out the material in many different ways before they set it for performance. I encourage the students to "see" the action in their heads and project that vision to the audience. They do not have to memorize the script, but they need to know it well if they are going to read it fluently and effectively to the rest of the class or to an outside group.

Inclusive Schools: An Observation Checklist

1. During unstructured times in your classrooms, how do students group themselves? Who is participating in which activities?

   _____

   _____

2. What kinds of activities are the girls involved in?

   _____

   _____

3. What kinds of activities are the boys involved in?

   _____

   _____

4. When there is conflict, what kind of language do you hear between the boys? Between the girls? Between the boys and girls?

   _____

   _____

5. Who appears to be the most comfortable and the least comfortable in class?

   _____

   _____

6. Is anyone being left out of discussions and activities?

   _____

   _____

7. Are the students aware of the exclusion of individuals or certain groups?

   _____

   _____

8. Do all students contribute equally to class discussions?

   _____

   _____

9. How do students function in small group discussions?

   _____

   _____

10. Which students are able to work independently?

_____

_____

11. How are English language learners integrated into the work that is taking place in the classroom?

_____

_____

12. How are Special Education students integrated in the classroom?

_____

_____

13. Are computers and other resources in the classroom shared equally?

_____

_____

14. Who are the students who usually volunteer to help you with your classroom organization?

_____

_____

15. Which students usually receive the most attention, praise, and/or criticism in class?

_____

_____

16. Do the curriculum and the classroom resources reflect the cultural/linguistic/racial diversity of your school community?

_____

_____

17. Which students have lunchtime issues (e.g., don't bring a lunch; don't eat lunch at all)?

_____

_____

18. Does the cafeteria serve the kind of food that reflects the diversity of the school community?

_____

_____

19. Is there a place in the school where students can pray?

_____

_____

20. Are physical education and health education activities co-ed?

_____

_____

21. Are parents, guardians, or other family members employed in the school? If so, who are these family members?

_____

_____

22. Do all parents/guardians/family members participate in the educational experiences of their children?

_____

_____

23. Are translation services provided to parents/guardians/family members?

_____

_____

24. Do all students have access to extracurricular activities?

_____

_____

Speech Bubble, Whisper Bubble, and Thought Bubble

Analyzing Family Relationships in Magazine Ads

	Student 1	Student 2
Number of people in the family		
What are the relationships amongst the family members?		
What does the family look like in terms of race?		
What does the family look like in terms of social class? How did you infer this?		
What product is being sold in the ad?		

Bibliography

Aboriginal Voices in the Curriculum: A Guide to Teaching Aboriginal Studies in K-8 Classrooms. 2003. Toronto District School Board.

Banks, James A. 1993. "Multicultural Education: Historical Development, Dimensions, and Practice." In *Review of Research into Education* 19 (1), 3-49.

Barth, Roland S. 1990. *Improving Schools from Within: Teachers, Parents and Principals Can Make the Difference.* San Francisco, CA: Jossey-Bass.

Bauer, Anne M., and Glenda Myree Brown. 2001. *Adolescents and Inclusion: Transforming Secondary Schools.* Baltimore, Maryland: Paul H. Brookes.

Bigelow, B., B. Harvey, S. Karp, and L. Miller, eds. 2001. *Rethinking Schools: Teaching for Equity and Social Justice.* Vol. 2. Milwaukee, WI: Rethinking Schools.

Binder, M. 2004. "The Importance of Child Art as a Foundation for Teaching and Learning." In *The Arts Go to School*, edited by D. Booth and M. Hachiya, pp. 35-38. Markham, ON: Pembroke.

Black, Paul and Dylan William. 1998. "Inside the Black Box: Raising Standards Through Classroom Assessment." In *Phi Delta Kappan*, pp. 139–48.

Boal, A. 1979. *Theatre of the Oppressed.* Trans. A. Jackson. London and New York: Routledge.

Booth, David. 2005. *Story Drama: Creating Stories Through Role Playing, Improvising, and Reading Aloud.* Markham, ON: Pembroke.

Booth, David W., and Charles J. Lundy. 1985. *Improvisation: Learning Through Drama.* Toronto: Harcourt Brace Jovanovich.

Booth, David, and K. Gallagher, eds. 2003. "Towards an Understanding of Theatre for Education." In *How Theatre Educates: Convergences and Counterpoints with Artists, Scholars, and Advocates.* Toronto: University of Toronto Press.

Booth, David W., and Kathleen Gould Lundy. 2006. *In Graphic Detail.* Toronto: Rubicon.

Campbell, Nicola I. 2006. *Shi-shi-etko.* Toronto: House of Anansi Press.

Christensen, Linda. 2000. *Reading, Writing and Rising Up: Teaching about Social Justice and the Power of the Written Word.* Milwaukee, WI: Rethinking Schools.

Courtney, Richard. 1989. *Play, Drama and Thought: The Intellectual Background to Dramatic Education.* Toronto: Simon and Pierre.

Delpit, Lisa. 2006. *Other People's Children: Cultural Conflict in the Classroom.* New York: The New Press.

Delpit, Lisa. 1988. "The Silenced Dialogue: Power and Pedagogy in Educating Other People's Children." In *Harvard Educational Review.* 58(3): 280-98.

Dippo, Don. 2005. "Redefining Community/Urban University Relations: A Project for Education Faculties?" In *Teaching Education* 16(2) (June), pp. 89–101.

Eisner, Elliot. 2002. *The Arts and Creation of Mind.* New Haven, CT: Yale University Press.

Equitable Schools: It's in Our Hands. Resources for School Leaders. 2005. Toronto District School Board.

Equity Foundation Statement and Commitments to Equity Policy and Implementation. 2000. Toronto District School Board.

Franco, Betty, ed. 2000. *You Hear Me? Poems and Writing by Teenage Boys.* New York: Candlewick Press.

Frank, Anne. 1993. *Anne Frank: the Diary of a Young Girl.* New York: Doubleday.

Freire, Paulo. 2001. *Pedagogy of Freedom: Ethics, Democracy and Civic Courage.* New York: Rowman and Littlefield.

Fry, Christopher. 1953. *A Sleep of Prisoners.* New York: Dramatists Play Service Inc.

Fullan, Michael. 1997. "Emotion and Hope: Constructive Concepts for Complex Times." ASCD: Rethinking Educational Change with Heart and Mind, pp. 216–233.

Gallagher, Kathleen. 2000. *Drama Education in the Lives of Girls.* Toronto: University of Toronto Press.

Gallagher, Kathleen, and David Booth, eds. 2003. *How Theatre Educates: Convergences and Counterpoints.* Toronto: University of Toronto Press.

Gallagher, Kathleen. 2007. *The Theatre of Urban: Youth and Schooling in Dangerous Times.* Toronto: University of Toronto Press.

Gardner, Howard. 1983. *Frames of Mind: The Theory of Multiple Intelligences.* New York: Basic Books.

Gardner, Howard. 2006. *Five Minds of the Future.* Boston: Harvard Business School Press.

Ghosh, Ratna. 2008. "Racism: A Hidden Curriculum." In *Education Canada* 48(4) (Fall): 26-29.

Goleman, Daniel. 1995. *Emotional Intelligence.* New York: Bantam Books.

Grady, Sharon. 2000. *Drama and Diversity: A Pluralistic Perspective for Educational Drama.* Portsmouth, NH: Heinemann.

Greder, Armin. 2007. *The Island.* Crows Nest, AU: Allen and Unwin.

Greene, M. 1995. *Releasing the Imagination: Essays on Education, the Arts and Social Change.* San Francisco, CA: Jossey-Bass.

Greene, Maxine. 2001. *Variations on a Blue Guitar. The Lincoln Center Institute Lectures on Aesthetic Education.* New York: Teachers College Press.

Hansberry, Lorraine. 2004. *A Raisin in the Sun.* New York: Random House.

Hargreaves, Andy, and Dean Fink. 2003. "The Seven Principles of Sustainable Leadership." In *Educational Leadership.* April, ASCD, 61(7):8–13.

Hearn, Emily, and Marywinn Milne, eds. 2007. *Our New Home: Immigrant Children Speak.* Toronto: Second Story Press.

Heathcote, Dorothy. 1980. *Drama as Context.* Great Britain: Aberdeen University Press, The National Association for the Teaching of English.

Heathcote, Dorothy, Cecily O'Neill, and Liz Johnson, eds. 1991. *Dorothy Heathcote: Collected Writings on Education and Drama.* Evanston, IL: Northwestern University Press.

Heck, M. L. 2001. "Eye Messages: A Partnership of Artmaking and Multicultural Education." In *Multicultural Perspectives* 3(1), 3-8.

Heschel, Abraham. 1996. *Moral Grandeur and Spiritual Audacity.* Essays edited by Susannah Heschel. New York: Farrar, Strauss and Giroux.

hooks, bell. 1994. *Teaching to Transgress: Education as the Practice of Freedom.* New York: Routledge.

_____. 2004. *Skin Again.* New York: Hyperion Books.

Hume, Karen. 2008. *Start Where They Are: Differentiating for Success with the Young Adolescent.* Toronto, ON: Pearson Education.

Jaine, Linda, ed. 1995. *Residential Schools: The Stolen Years.* Saskatoon, SK: University Extension Press.

James, Carl E. 2004. "Assimilation to Accommodation: Immigrants and the Changing Patterns of Schooling." In *Education Canada* 44(4). CBCA Education.

James, Carl E. 2004. "Urban Education: An Approach to Community-based Education." In *Intercultural Education* 15(1): 15–32.

Keith, Kent. 2001. *Anyway: The Paradoxical Commandments—Finding Personal Meaning in a Crazy World*. New York: G.P. Putnam and Sons.

Kingsolver, Barbara. 1990. *Animal Dreams*. New York: Harper Collins.

Lowry, Lois. 1993. *The Giver*. New York: Random House Children's Books.

Lundy, Kathleen Gould. 2006. *In a Class of Her Own*. Toronto: Rubicon.

Lundy, Kathleen Gould and Joan Green. 2005. "Wedding Album." In *Family Ties*. Oakville, Ontario: Rubicon.

Lundy, Kathleen Gould, Christine Jackson, Lorna Wilson, and Lorraine Sutherns. 2001. *The Treasure Chest: Story, Drama and Dance/Movement in the Classroom*. Toronto: Toronto District School Board.

Maathi, Wangari Muta. 2007. *Unbowed: A Memoir*. New York: Anchor Books, Random House.

Mackenzie, Judith. 1993. "Letter." In *Values: The Issues Collection*. Whitby, ON: McGraw-Hill Ryerson.

Martinez, Alejandro Cruz. 1991. *The Woman Who Outshone the Sun. La Mujer que brillaba aun mas que el sol*. San Francisco: Children's Book Press.

McIntosh, P. 2000. "White Privilege: Unpacking the Invisible Knapsack." In *Gender Through the Prism of Difference*, 2nd Edition, pp. 247-50. M. B. Zinn, P. Hondagneu-Sotelo, and M. A. Messner, eds. Boston: Allyn and Bacon.

Miller, Debbie. 2008. *Teaching with Intention: Defining Beliefs, Aligning Practice, Taking Action, K-5*. Markham, ON: Pembroke.

Mitchell, Adrian. 2004. *Nobody Rides the Unicorn*. New York: Arthur A. Levine Books.

Moban-Uddin, Asma. 2005. *My Name is Bilal*. Honesdale, Pennsylvania: Boyds Mill Press.

Morgan, Norah, and Juliana Saxton. 2006. *Asking Better Questions*, 2nd Edition. Markham, ON: Pembroke.

Morrison, Toni. 1992. *Playing in the Dark: Whiteness and the Literary Imagination*. Cambridge: Harvard University Press.

Neelands, Jonothan. 1984. *Making Sense of Drama: A Guide to Classroom Practice*. London: Heinemann.

Neelands, Jonothan, and Tony Goode, eds. 1992. *Structuring Drama Work: A Handbook of Available Forms in Theatre and Drama*. Cambridge: Cambridge University Press.

Palmer, Patrick. 2007. *The Courage to Teach: Exploring the Inner Landscape of a Teacher's Life*. San Francisco, CA: Jossey-Bass.

Pitt, Alice, and Deborah Britzman. 2006. "Speculations on Qualities of Difficult Knowledge in Teaching and Learning." In *Doing Educational Research: A Handbook*, pp. 379-402 by Kenneth George Tobin, and J. Kincheloe. Sense Publishers.

Pollock, Sharon. 1978. *The Komagata Maru Incident*. Toronto: Playwrights Co-op.

Pomerance, Bernard. 1979. *The Elephant Man*. New York: Grove Press.

Probst, Robert. 1988. "Dialogue with a Text." In *The English Journal*, Vol. 77, No 1. National Council of Teachers of English, pp. 32-38.

Rainbows and Triangles: A Curriculum Document for Challenging Homophobia and Heterosexism in the K-6 Classroom. 2002. Toronto District School Board.

Schniedewind, Nancy, and Ellen Davidson. 1998. *Open Minds to Equality. A Sourcebook of Learning Activities to Affirm Diversity and Promote Equity*. Needham Heights, MA: Allyn and Bacon.

Soloman, Patrick, and Dia N.R. Sekay, eds. 2007. *Urban Teacher Education and Teaching: Innovative Practices for Diversity and Social Justice*. London and New York: Routledge.

Souster, Raymond, 1984. *Collected Poems of Raymond Souster*. Ottawa: Oberon Press.

Swartz, Larry. 2002. *The New Dramathemes*, 3rd Edition. Markham, ON: Pembroke.

Tan, Shaun. 2006. *The Arrival.* New York: Arthur A. Levine Books.

Vygotsky, L.S. 1987. "Imagination and Its Development in Childhood." In R. W. Rieber and A. S. Carion, eds. *The Collected Works of L. S. Vygotsky.* (1): 339-349. New York: Plenum Press.

Wagner, B. J. 1999. *Dorothy Heathcote: Drama as a Learning Medium.* Portland, MA: Calendar Islands Publishers.

Wagner, Betty Jane. 1999. "Attitudes, Behavior, and Moral Reasoning." In B. Wagner, ed. *Building Moral Communities Through Educational Drama,* pp. 137-156. Stamford, CN: Ablex.

Waite, Terry. 1994. *Taken On Trust.* Toronto: Seal Books, McClelland-Bantam.

Wheatley, Margaret. 1992. *Turning to One Another: Simple Conversations to Restore Hope to the Future.* San Francisco: Barrett-Koehler.

Willinsky, John. 1998. *Learning to Divide the World: Education at Empire's End.* Minneapolis: University of Minnesota Press.

Yolen, Jane. 1992. *Encounter.* Orlando, Florida: Harcourt Brace and Company.

Zatzman, Belarie. 2003. "The Monologue Project: Drama as a Form of Witnessing." In *How Theatre Educates: Convergences and Counterpoints with Artists, Scholars, and Advocates,* edited by K. Gallagher and D. Booth. Toronto: University of Toronto Press, pp. 35-55.

Zatzman, Belarie. 2005. "Staging History: Aesthetics and the Performance of Memory." In Special Issue: Aesthetics in Drama and Theatre Education, *The Journal of Aesthetic Education,* Volume 39, Number 4, pp. 96-104.

Zatzman, Belarie. 2008. "Fifty-one Suitcases: Traces of Hana Brady and the Terezin Children." In Special Issue: Children and Theatre, *Canadian Theatre Review,* 133, pp. 28-37.

Index

Active engagement
    Interpreting text through, 89–125
Active hope, 129
Analyzing family relationships in magazine ads, 150
    Planning and teaching with students in mind, 64
    Talking ourselves into understanding, 63–64
    Writing in role as an object, 62
Angelica-Leslie, 96–102
    Creating a protected bower of analysis, 97–98
    Prepared improvisation, 99–100
    Questioning in role, 98–99
    Reconnecting to the real story, 101–102
    Role-playing, 100–101
Architecture of the imagination, 60–64
Artifacts, 90–92, 141
The Arrival, 64–69
    Creating a story through chamber theatre, 60
    If pictures could talk, 68–69, 137

Biases
    Systemic, 12
Brainstorming, 82, 85, 107, 141
Bursting the bubble, 73, 137

Chamber theatre, 69, 138
Character, 13
    Developing, 13, 37
Choral speaking, 145
Class discussion, 106
Classrooms of conscience, 89
Cognitive capabilities, 24
Collaboration, 27–28, 130
Collaborative art installation, 135
Collegiality, 27–28, 130–131
Community

Building, 32–51
Caring, 89
Conscience, 134
Creating, 33,
    Getting to know, 32–33
    Interactions with school, 33
Critical pedagogy, 110
Critical questioning, 76, 139
Critical thinking / awareness, 53, 55, 64, 82
    Emotional literacy and, 52–88
Curriculum
    Heroes and heroine, 26
    Inclusive, 8, 23–31, 36–51, 131
    Windows, mirrors, and doors, 57–58

The Diary of Anne Frank, 121–125
Drama, 53
    Anti-racist education through, 56, 57–58
    Bearing witness, 55
    Circular, 110–112, 144
    Empathy and point of view, 53–54
    Equity education, 56–58
    Exploring silent voices through, 54–55
    Finding our voices through, 54
    Immersion in, 53
    Involvement in, 53
    Language, 54
    Provoking conversations, 55
    Strategies in education, 53
    Unknown possibilities, 55

The Elephant Man, 110–114
    Circular drama, 110–112
    Prepared scenes, 112–113
    Split-second scenes, 112

This is your line, 113–114
   Voices in the head, 112
Emotional literacy, 53, 79
   Critical thinking and, 52–88
Emotions
   Sequencing, 105
Empathy, 102
Encounter, 82–88
   Brainstorming, 85
   Deciphering the story, myth, or message, 84–85
   Evaluation, 85
   Interpreting the story, myth, or message, 84
   Reading out loud, 85–86
   Reflection, 86
   Revisiting the dream, 86–88
Environment for learning, 36–51
   Cooperative games, 38, 40–41
   Rules of engagement, 37–38
Equality, 24–25
Equity, 24–25
   Education, 56–58
   Games that focus on inclusion and, 41–51
   Graphic novels and teaching about, 71–74
   Using metaphors in education, 57–58
Expectations, 36

Fairness, 8
   Characteristics of, 10
   Distinguishing from unfairness, 12–14
   Teaching, 8, 9, 10, 21
   Working toward, 37
Fears, 75–76
Feedback, 37–38, 127
Flocking, 139–140
Forum theatre, 106, 119, 143–144
Four Times Story Nouns, 65–67, 136

Games
   Atom, 40
   Back to Back/Face to Face, 40
   Birthday Line, 40
   Concentric Circles, 41–42
   Concentric Circles in Role, 42–43
   Cooperative, 38, 40–41, 134
   Equity and inclusion, 41–51
   Expert, 135
   Hearing the Absent Voices, 43–44
   Heigh Ho!, 41
   I am From… / We are From…, 44–48, 134
   Lay Your Cards on the Table, 48–51, 134
   Let Me Introduce You To…, 44
   Name, 135
   Name Switch Now, 41

Say Hello, 38
Sushi, 41
The Seat on My Right Is Free, 40
Who Are We? Where Are We?, 43
The Giver, 75–79
   Critical questioning, 76
   Interviewing in role, 76–78
   Making lists, 75–76
   Map-making, 75
   Out-of-role reflection, 79
   Questioning in role, 78
   Writing in role, 78–79
Graphic novels, 70–74
   Characteristics, 70, 71
   Description, 70
   Developing literacy through, 70–71
   Teaching about equity, 71–74

Hieroglyphics, 83, 141
Homophobia, 114
Hot seating, 119–120, 144

Identity, 48–51
   Description, 48, 49
   Feelings associated with inclusion/exclusion, 50
   Images of, 48–51
Imagining and hoping, 39
Improvisation, 141
   Prepared, 99–100, 143
   Spontaneous, 139–140, 141
   Telephone conversations, 106
In a Class of Her Own, 70–74
   Developing literacy through graphic novels, 70–71
   Graphic novels and teaching about equity, 71–74
Inclusive classroom
   Strategies to use in, 134–145
Inclusive curriculum, 8, 23–31, 131
   Collegiality and collaboration, 27–28
   Courageous leadership, 27
   Equitable school environment, 25–27
   Establishing and sustaining, 24
   Goal, 24
   Imagining yourself forward, 29–31, 36
   Inclusive, respectful environment for learning, 36–51
   Mentorship, 28–29
   Multi-faceted perspective, 24
Inclusive schools: observation checklist, 146–148
Instant choreography, 84
The Island, 92–96
   Comparing and contrasting pictures, 93–94
   Drawing and writing, 95
   Entry points: responding to images, 93–95
   Other writing techniques, 96

Staging tableaux, 94–95
Story/word punctuation, 94

Language
    Models of, 113–114
Leadership, 27, 28
    Capacity, 130
    Courageous, 27
Learning, 36
    Establish an inclusive, respectful environment for,
        36–51
"Letter", 106–110
    Documentary scene, 109
    Inner/outer circle, 108
    Is there such a thing as a second chance?, 109–110
    Lost key stories, 109
Listening, 8, 38

Making lists, 75–76, 139
Making predictions, 81
"The Man Who Finds That His Son Has Become a Thief",
    102–106
    Asking questions out of role, 103
    Class discussion, 106
    Forum theatre, 106
    Improvised telephone conversations, 106
    Parallel universes, 104
    Partner work, 105
    Reading and understanding the poem, 104–105
    Reading for clarification, 103
    Sequencing emotions, 105
    Tableaux, 104
    Teacher in role, 102–103
    Writing in role, 104
Map-making, 75, 139
Mentors, 28–29
Metaphors
    Dry winding riverbed, 58, 60
    Using in equity education, 57–58
    Windows, mirrors, and doors, 57–59
Miniature sets, 61, 135

Nobody Rides the Unicorn, 79–82
    Before reading, 80
    Brainstorming, 82
    During reading, 80–81
    Making predictions, 81
    Voices in the head, 81–82

Overheard conversations, 145

Parallel universes, 104, 143
Partner work, 105

Pictures
    Comparing and contrasting, 93–94
    If pictures could move, 137
    If pictures could talk, 68–69, 137
    Magazine, 115–116
    Rearranging, 116–119, 144
    Stepping in and out of, 142–143
Principals
    Openness, 28
Professional learning communities, 128, 130–131
Protected bower of analysis, 97, 102
Punctuation
    Story/word, 94, 142

Questioning
    Critical, 76, 139
    In role, 78

Readers Theatre, 145
Reading, 70
    Clarification, 103
    Inner/outer circle, 74, 108, 138–139
    Modeled, 72, 138
    Out loud, 85–86
    Small groups, 71, 73
    Walk around, 145
Residential Schools: The Stolen Years, 90–92
Respect, 37
Role
    Asking questions out of, 103
    Interviewing in, 76–78, 136
    Questioning in, 78, 98–99
    Reflection out of, 79
    Teacher in, 102–103, 143
    Writing in, 78–79, 98–99, 104, 120–121, 136–137
Role-playing, 86, 100–101, 102, 108, 136
Roles on the wall, 71–73, 91, 138
Rules of engagement, 37, 120

Scenes
    Prepared, 112–113
    Split-second, 112, 144
School
    Environment, 25–27
    New beginnings, 33–35
School board policies, 11
School environment
    Cafeteria, 25
    Hallways, 25
    Inclusive and equitable, 25–27
    School library, 25
    School office, 26
School learning project, 15–22

Sculpture garden, 136
Silent voices, 53, 54–55, 60
Situated encounters, 113
Statues, 135–136
Storytelling, 138
Students
  Active engagement, 48
  Behavior, 37
  Challenges faced by, 12
  Challenging, 37
  Critical awareness, 52
  Drama, 53–54
  Drama message, 18–20
  Educating to be good citizens, 13–14
  Engaging the disengaged, 127
  Ethical citizens, 12
  Exploring identity, 48–51
  Gaining trust of, 9
  Games, 38
  Group-building activities, 37
  Learning about, 31
  Location, 9
  Piquing interest of, 70
  Protecting into understanding, 51
  Recognizing and meeting needs of, 11
  Relationships with, 36, 37
  Sense of themselves, 21–22
  Sharing, 41
  Supporting, 36–37, 132
  Uncovering assumptions about human differences, 102
  Unlocking future of, 11–12
  Valuing, 26
  Working with, 53

Tableaux, 104, 109, 110, 142
  Staging, 94–95
Teaching (teachers)
  Anti-discriminatory, 127
  Building respect, 37
  Challenges, 31
  Class discussion, 106
  Constructing together, 131–133
  Context, 129
  Critical awareness, 52
  Developing classroom relationships, 24–25
  Developing flexible frames of mind, 127
  Disposition, 14–15
  Educating students on being good people, 13–14
  Effective, 35–36
  Equity and social justice, 56
  Examining dominant class-based power dynamics, 106–107
  Fairness, 8, 9, 10, 21

Homophobia, 114
Imagining yourself forward, 29–31, 36
Impact of, 129
Inclusive classrooms, 29
Keeping expectations high, 36
Keeping students in mind, 64
Learning what to control, 131
Linking personal narratives and material, 64–65
Making a difference, 14–15
Motivating discouraged readers, 70
Piquing interest of students, 70
Power of, 9
Relationships, 28, 36, 37
Rethinking core beliefs, 9–10
Sense of students, 21–22, 31
Six Es, 35–36
Successful, 14–15
Supporting students, 36–37, 132
Unshackling thought, 55
Valuing students, 26
Working with students, 53
Thinking
  Possibility, 12
  Poverty, 12
  Probability, 12
This is your line, 113–114, 144
Transformation, 20–21
The Treasure Chest project, 58–59
True wisdom, 97

Voiceover, 95, 139
Voices in the head, 112, 141

The wave, 140
"Wedding Album", 114–121
  Forum theatre, 119
  Hot seating, 119–120
  Rearranging the pictures, 116–119
  Working with magazine images, 115–116
  Writing in role, 120–121
The Woman Who Outshone the Sun, 58–60
  Inclusion/exclusion, 59–60
Writing
  Alternative endings, 96
  Diary entries, 96
  Drawing and, 95, 143
  In role, 78–79, 98–99, 104, 120–121, 136–137
  Letters, 96
  Message in a bottle, 96
  Modeled, 140
  Reading out, 74, 138–139
  Research similar stories, 96
  Techniques, 96

Acknowledgments

I wish to acknowledge all the teachers and principals who have invited me into their classrooms and schools over the years to work with their students. I appreciate the time that was set aside to allow me to do the kind of teaching that I love to do and for all of the conversations—both in person, through email, and over the telephone—about what transpired in the various classrooms and about what could have happened differently if other teaching choices had been made. I have learned so much by engaging in what I call critical "unpacking" of conversations that move the work forward beyond superficial understandings of the teaching and learning dynamic.

I extend thanks as well to the members of the Equity Studies Department at the Toronto Board of Education, who recognized at a very early stage the critical connection between drama and inclusive education. They started me on my journey toward understanding what needs to happen so that schools can be safe, effective, and equitable. The Canadian Education Association gave me an opportunity that forever altered my perceptions about what schools can do to "get things right" for adolescent learners in contemporary classrooms. I cannot thank them enough for inviting me to be the Artistic Director of the "Imagine a School..." project.

My students and colleagues at York University continue to challenge me to think in new ways about arts and equity education. I am so privileged to work at a university that cares so much about social justice and the work that needs to be done in schools, in communities, and in the university itself.

And as one final note of gratitude, many Canadians miss Peter Gzowki's brilliance as an interviewer on CBC radio. He had the uncanny gift to help us tell our stories in compelling ways. It gives me enormous pleasure to include a letter to him by Judith MacKenzie that was shared with listeners of his "Morningside" program many years ago.

Sources of material used in this book. Every effort has been made to contact copyright holders for permission to reproduce borrowed material. The publishers apologize for any such omissions and will be pleased to rectify them in subsequent reprints of the book.

"A Life Worth Living" was written by Quantedius Hall.

Patten, Brian. "Minister for Exams." Reproduced by permission of the author c/o Rodgers, Coleridge and White Ltd., 20 Powls Mews, London W11 1JN.

"What Do We Do with a Variation?" is reprinted with permission from James Berry's book *Only One of Me: Selected Poems*, published by Macmillan Children's Books, UK.

Excerpts from *Residential Schools: The Stolen Years* are reprinted with permission of University Extension Press, The University of Saskatchewan.

"The Paradoxical Commandments" are reprinted by permission of the author, Kent M. Keith. (c) Copyright Kent M. Keith 1968, renewed 2001.